AN
INVITATION
TO
SEE

AN INVITATION TO SEE

125 PAINTINGS FROM THE MUSEUM OF MODERN ART

INTRODUCTION AND
COMMENTS BY
HELEN M. FRANC

THE MUSEUM
OF MODERN ART
NEW YORK

Copyright © 1973 by The Museum of Modern Art
All rights reserved
Library of Congress Catalog Card Number 72-82887
Paperbound ISBN 0-87070-230-0
Cloth Binding ISBN 0-87070-231-9

Designed by Carl Laanes
Type set by York Graphic Services, Inc., York, Pennsylvania
Printed by Lebanon Valley Offset, Inc., Annville, Pennsylvania
Bound by Sendor Bindery, Inc., New York, New York

The Museum of Modern Art
11 West 53 Street, New York, New York 10019
Printed in the United States of America

Fourth Printing, 1979

CONTENTS

To the Public of The Museum of Modern Art

THE TITLE OF THIS BOOK, like many of the ideas it contains, is taken from Alfred H. Barr, Jr. In his introduction to *Masters of Modern Art,* published in 1954 on the occasion of the Twenty-fifth Anniversary of The Museum of Modern Art, Mr. Barr wrote: "Today [the Museum's collection] numbers many thousands of works of art. A few of the best or most characteristic are reproduced here, more to give pleasure than for any systematic exposition or record. Even more, this picture-book is an invitation to see the originals!"

This more modest book deals only with paintings; it reproduces and comments upon one hundred and twenty-five from among more than two thousand now in the collection. The choice has not been easy. Certain paintings would without doubt be included in any selection, but the respective claims of others are more difficult to assess. Every reader will therefore find here some of his favorites, wonder why others have been omitted, and perhaps encounter a few not previously known to him. Similarly, because space in the Museum's galleries, like the format of this book, is necessarily limited, on any one occasion the visitor will find on view a majority, but not all, of the pictures included here. The remainder, if not on loan, may be seen in the Study Center.

The principal criterion of selection has been to choose works that individually are of outstanding quality or significance, and that collectively demonstrate the remarkable diversity of styles and approaches characteristic of the modern achievement in painting. As Mr. Barr pointed out, this diversity is the result of differences among artists that "are real and significant, slowly developed, passionately believed in, and expressive not simply of artistic convictions but often of deeply felt philosophies of life."

This book is not intended to be an historical survey, and it does not attempt to define and trace the successive styles and movements within modern art. Its organization is somewhat unconventional. Though most of the earlier works will be found at the beginning, and the more recent toward the end, there are exceptions to that order, and throughout most of the book pictures are paired or arranged in sequences that disregard chronology and immediate stylistic or historical affiliations.

As the title indicates, the book is "an invitation to see." Its purpose is to focus attention on the individual paintings reproduced. Perception of the qualities in a work of art can sometimes be made more acute by comparing or contrasting it with another, with which it may share certain similarities while differing in other respects. It is such likenesses and differences—in subject matter, style, technique, and overall content—that are emphasized here. These comparisons are meant merely to be suggestive; except when specifically noted, they should not be taken as implying a direct connection between one work, or one artist, and another.

No reproduction, of course, can ever be more than a souvenir of the original, as a photograph is of a living person. With respect to color, printer's ink can only approximate the artist's pigment. The differences in texture between the heavy impasto of van Gogh's *Starry Night* and the even surface of Albers' *Homage to the Square: Broad Call,* for example, can only be suggested. Coated paper gives a uniform finish to all the reproductions, whereas in actuality some paintings are glossy, others mat, and still others (such as Pollock's *One*) deliberately exploit the contrast between these two qualities. But the greatest distortion of all is in scale. No illustration in this book is more than $5\frac{5}{8}$ inches high; the originals, however, range from Dali's diminutive *Persistence of Memory,* measuring $9\frac{1}{2}$ by 13 inches, to Newman's wall-size *Vir Heroicus Sublimis,* almost 8 feet high by 18 feet long. Obviously, much of a painting's impact depends upon the spectator's kinesthetic response to its dimensions. The measurements of each work are given here, so that the reader can know its true size and recollect or imagine the effect it produces.

There is a distinction between "seeing" and "looking." As we walk down the street, a host of images impinges on our sight; we "see" but are not really conscious of many of these visual impressions. Prudence advises us, however, that when we reach the corner, we should "look" at the traffic light—is it red or green? Within the gallery of a museum, we are confronted simultaneously by many works of art. It takes an effort of will to stop before any single one long enough to examine it searchingly. Yet it is only after such focusing of the attention that we can really be said to "see" more than the superficial aspects of a painting.

Aware of the size of a collection or exhibition, and the limits of time at his disposal, the visitor is apt to enter the first gallery, pass around it, and then proceed to the next. Soon the familiar phenomenon known as museum fatigue sets in; and even before his feet begin to bother him, his eyes and mind feel taxed by the many demands upon them, his attention slackens, and his enjoyment gradually ebbs.

But, when all is said and done, there really is no reason other than enjoyment for spending an hour or so looking at works of art—or reproductions of them—rather than reading a book, going to the movies, visiting friends, playing golf or tennis, or engaging in any of the other diversions for which most of us find all too little time. It is true that the charter of 1929 states that The Museum of Modern Art had been established "for the purpose of encouraging and developing the study of modern arts and the application of such arts to manufacture and practical life, and furnishing popular instruction"; a little later, this purpose was more succinctly defined as "helping people to use, understand, and enjoy the visual arts of our time." Today, however, these formulations seem to carry the overtones of being survivals of the nineteenth century's firm commitment to the utilitarian, and possibly even of its pious and optimistic belief that works of art can elevate man's mind and so improve his moral character—a proposition hardly susceptible of proof. Moreover, one of the delights of art is precisely that it is gratuitous, with no demonstrable practical application whatever. As for "understanding," inasmuch as artists themselves have sometimes confessed that they did not wholly comprehend their own creations (see, for example, Pollock's remarks on *The She-Wolf,* page 83, or Beckmann's on his *Departure,* pages 104–105), it is probably presumptuous to believe that we can do so. In addition, there is Picasso's quelling observation: "Everyone wants to understand art. Why not try to understand the song of a bird? Why does one love the night, flowers, everything around one, without trying to understand it? But in the case of painting people have to *understand.* If only they would realize above all that an artist works because he must, that he himself is only a trifling bit of the world, and that no more importance should be attached to him than to plenty of other things in the world which please us, though we can't explain them."

With Picasso's authorization, then (and that of the Declaration of Independence, which recognizes "the pursuit of happiness" as one of man's inalienable rights), let us freely allow ourselves to look at paintings for sheer delight. With this in mind, I venture to suggest that the visitor's enjoyment may be greater if he refrain from plodding from picture to picture in a systematic fashion. I recommend that he try the experiment of entering a gallery, glancing around it, fixing on the painting that most immediately attracts him, and making a beeline toward it; and that he then spend a few minutes in leisurely investigation of it before passing on to another, chosen in the same fashion.

Enjoyment, of course, can be of different sorts. Sometimes we want to listen to Bach, at other times to Tchaikowsky; today we feel in the mood for an Ingmar Bergman film, tomorrow for one of Chaplin's. The tremendous variety within the Museum's collection of paintings can hardly fail to offer something for our pleasure. Even among the limited selections in this book, one can find subjects as traditional as portraits, landscapes, cityscapes, still lifes, allegories, religious themes, and political topics. There are figurative paintings of many sorts, and examples of the many kinds of abstraction that have evolved in this century. There are everyday scenes transformed into poetry by the artist's view of them, fantasies that exist only in his imagination, and paintings that try to make visible what is unseen, such as the fourth dimension or the hidden processes of nature. Some pictures reflect a tragic view of life, others extol its joys; some are grave and serious, some satirical, some humorous. The handling of the medium may reveal the artist's intense emotion, the working of his unconscious impulses, or a strict discipline imposed by his intellect. Paint may be heaped up into heavy clots on the surface of the canvas, soaked into it, applied in dots, or laid on with unvarying smoothness. Color ranges from monochrome to many-hued radiance. The conventional rules of perspective may be carefully followed, distorted, or ignored; or spatial recession within a painting may be denied altogether.

In proposing that the viewer be guided first of all by his personal preference, I by no means imply that he should be content to react like litmus paper, instantly deciding "I like—don't like." Initial response to a painting should be a starting point and not a finish line. It should lead not only to a more prolonged scrutiny but also to the posing of questions. Just what is it in this picture that seems so pleasing? (Subject alone can be a snare, for the same theme might be execrably treated.) Is it the color? the light? the conveying of the artist's emotion? the sense of movement, or of absolute calm? the handling of paint? the forms themselves, or their decorative arrangement and the relationships among them? the play of lines, or the indication of volume? the impression of intimacy, or of grandeur and monumentality? fidelity to observed fact, or its transformation? Above all, how has the artist gone about achieving his effects?

Nowadays we are besieged with countless images of all kinds—in newspapers and magazines, on billboards and TV screens. We are accustomed to looking at most of them primarily for the information they impart; our eyes and minds are conditioned to comprehend "what" the message is, without pausing to analyze "how" it is stated. But painting's former function of providing information has largely been taken over by the photograph. Furthermore, modern painting seldom has the office of celebrating established religion or civil authority, and only rarely does it deal with traditional subjects by means of widely accepted conventions. Painting has become increasingly concerned with *how* it makes its statement; the quantum of its total content that depends on form rather than on any ostensible subject is proportionately greater than in the past.

Yet painting does not speak some arcane language that we need special skill to master. As children, we all responded to its basic elements of colors, lines, and shapes; but age and sophistication tend to blunt that uninhibited perceptiveness. The art of seeing art lies in retaining the child's ability to respond simply and directly, and tempering this with the adult's capacity for more concentrated attention and philosophical inquiry.

Sometimes extraneous facts intrude upon our faculty of observation. We are flooded with data about artists and movements, ranging from gossip-column items to erudite criticism, and these may color our view or prevent us from seeing what lies right before our eyes. The late René d'Harnoncourt, former Director of The Museum of Modern Art, used to tell an anecdote about his teaching days. He gave his students the assignment of visiting an exhibition of van Gogh's paintings, shortly after the publication of Irving Stone's fictionalized biography of that artist, *Lust for Life*. The class came back, reporting in detail how certain works reflected van Gogh's mental illness or foretold his suicide; but when asked to describe the predominant colors in those pictures, the students were unable to do so.

Once having examined a painting with care and tried to determine what in it particularly attracts him, the visitor might next seek out others that share those features. In the course of this quest, he may encounter works that he finds equally appealing, though they display quite different characteristics. He may even discover that some pictures that at first sight were little to his liking, or had nothing to say to him, merit after all his respectful attention, if not his unqualified favor. Frequently a painting that attracts us immediately soon begins to seem over-obvious and boring, while another that at first sight seemed "difficult" may in the long run afford us more lasting pleasure. Not only do our tastes change, in art as in everything else, but also the appetite for looking at paintings usually increases with practice. It may be likened to a spectator sport: the more we see our favorite game, the more we are able to appreciate its strategies and distinguish among the styles of the various players and teams. We become actively committed partisans rather than passive onlookers.

The comments accompanying the reproductions in this book are not meant to be either limiting or comprehensive. Their purpose is to clear away obstacles (as by identifying a subject or explaining a puzzling title), point out features that may be overlooked, or suggest ways of looking that in some instances may be applica-ble to other paintings also. Facts about the artists' lives and careers, and the discussion of movements, have been kept to a minimum and included only when of special pertinence to the particular work. Reading about art can widen our knowledge and, by illuminating certain aspects of it, add another dimension to our enjoyment; but it can no more be a substitute for the experience of seeing than reading the program notes for a symphony can be for the act of listening to it.

In some cases, the comments cite formulations by other critics; more frequently, the artists themselves have been quoted. What artists have to say about their work is almost always interesting but not necessarily conclusive, and is often baffling. "The truth is, we can only make our pictures speak," van Gogh wrote in his last letter, just before his death. Apart from the difficulty that anyone has in being objective about himself, there are semantic ambiguities. Leaving aside the fact that Rousseau and Hirshfield both thought of themselves as "realistic" painters, how confusing it is to discover that whereas some artists regard their pictures as being "real" to the extent that they offer an accurate transcription of observed phenomena, conversely others hold their paintings to be "real" precisely because they contain no reference to anything that exists outside the works' own material substance. Monet tried to be true to nature by recording as exactly as he could the color, light, and forms he observed in his water garden. Klee and Newman, on the other hand, did not attempt to depict what can be seen in nature but rather to emulate in their paintings the creative forces whereby nature brings order out of chaos. How many different meanings, also, have attached themselves to the words "abstract" and "abstraction"! And how surprising to know that when Malevich, van Doesburg, and Mondrian purged their art of any imitation of forms occurring in the real world, they were not seeking to be hermetic but, on the contrary, to develop a universal language that eventually could be understood by all.

Instead of indulging in mere solipsistic self-expression, as has sometimes been alleged, the modern artist does in fact work for the public, as did artists of the past. His task in communicating, however, may be more difficult than formerly. He seldom works on commission, so his potential patron is usually unknown to him. There are no longer fixed traditions governing subject matter, iconography, style, and technique. Like nearly everything else in modern life, art is in a constant state of flux, with change proceeding at a more accelerated rate than at any previous time in history. The public for art is wider than ever before and is exposed to a glut of art, in the original and in reproduction. Consequently, it may be fickle in its allegiances, likening

9

art to fashion and demanding novelty rather than respecting true innovation; on the other hand, it may cling to what it already knows and be affronted by any sudden change in direction.

What is rejected today may nevertheless find acceptance tomorrow, or possibly be appreciated for qualities quite different from those for which it first won favor. In the long run, the role of the public is indispensable. This was recognized even by Marcel Duchamp, whose body of work is probably as abstruse as any ever produced. In a speech made in 1957, he said:

"In the last analysis, the artist may shout from all the rooftops that he is a genius; he will have to wait for the verdict of the spectator in order that his declarations take a social value and that, finally, posterity includes him in the primers of Art History. . . .

"In the creative act, the artist goes from intention to realization through a chain of totally subjective reactions. His struggle toward the realization is a series of efforts, pains, satisfactions, refusals, decisions, which also cannot and must not be fully self-conscious, at least on the aesthetic plane.

"The result of this struggle is a difference between the intention and its realization, a difference which the artist is not aware of. . . .

"The creative act takes another aspect when the spectator experiences the phenomenon of transmutation: through the change from inert matter into a work of art, an actual transubstantiation has taken place, and the role of the spectator is to determine the weight of the work on the aesthetic scale.

"All in all, the creative act is not performed by the artist alone; the spectator brings the work in contact with the external world by deciphering and interpreting its inner qualifications and thus adds his contribution to the creative act."

If the modern artist has more difficulties than artists of the past, in part because his freedom opens so many options to him, the modern public, too, has problems peculiar to our time in fulfilling its essential role of spectator and ultimate arbiter. That a pluralistic society has predictably given birth to many contradictory forms of art coexisting simultaneously is bewildering in itself.

Certainly, the artist does not deliberately seek mystification. Van Gogh, whose art never found acceptance in his lifetime, and whose paintings convey the perturbation of his highly intense, emotional sensibility, wrote in 1888: "In a picture I want to say something comforting as music is comforting." Similarly, in 1908, when Matisse's radical departures from natural color and form were still shocking to most of the public, he wrote: "What I dream of is an art of balance, of purity and serenity devoid of troubling or depressing subject matter, an art which might be for every mental worker, be he businessman or writer, like an appeasing influence, like a mental soother, something like a good armchair in which to rest from physical fatigue."

Writing half a century later, in the midst of the Age of Anxiety, the critic Leo Steinberg is not content to allow modern art, the artist, or the viewer so relaxed and hedonistic a role. He says:

"Contemporary art is constantly inviting us to applaud the destruction of values which we still cherish, while the positive cause, for the sake of which the sacrifices are made, is rarely made clear. . . .

"Modern art always projects itself into a twilight zone where no values are fixed. It is always born in anxiety. . . . It seems to me a function of modern art to transmit this anxiety to the spectator, so that his encounter with the work is—at least while the work is new—a genuine and existential predicament. . . . And we the public, artists included, should be proud of being in this predicament, because nothing else would seem to us quite true to life, and art, after all, is supposed to be a mirror of life."

Each viewer, then, is free to make his own choice. He can find good authority for allowing himself to contemplate art in order to seek refuge from the everyday problems that beset him, or for regarding it as an intensification of modern man's most anguishing concerns. Fortunately, his choice need not be an either-or, once-and-for-all decision. The paintings remain, to be visited and revisited, inviting his exploration and awaiting his changes of mood, his growth in perception.

Art, like poetry, speaks in metaphors, and poets have frequently been among those most sensitively attuned to its language. Let us, then, give the last word to Marianne Moore:

WHEN I BUY PICTURES
or what is closer to the truth,
when I look at that of which I may regard myself
*   as the imaginary possessor,*
I fix upon what would give me pleasure
*   in my average moments:*
. . . .
Too stern an intellectual emphasis upon
*   this quality or that detracts from one's enjoyment.*
It must not wish to disarm anything;
*   nor may the approved triumph easily be honored—*
that which is great because something else is small.
It comes to this: of whatever sort it is,
it must be "lit with piercing glances
*   into the life of things";*
it must acknowledge the spiritual forces
*   which have made it.*

125 PAINTINGS
FROM THE MUSEUM
OF MODERN ART

IN DIMENSIONS, height precedes width, followed in a few cases by a third dimension, depth. Accession numbers are enclosed in brackets, the two digits after the decimal point indicating the year in which the painting was acquired by The Museum of Modern Art.

HENRI ROUSSEAU. French, 1844–1910. *The Sleeping Gypsy.* 1897. Oil on canvas, 51 inches x 6 feet 7 inches. Gift of Mrs. Simon Guggenheim. [646.39]

"Night and silence! who is here?" Puck's query might well serve as rubric for this mysterious painting. Rousseau, a self-taught artist, thought of himself as a realist and sought to emulate such nineteenth-century academicians as Gérôme, who was famous for pictures of wild animals in bare stretches of African landscape. When Rousseau offered *The Sleeping Gypsy* to his native town Laval, he called it a "genre painting" and described its subject: "A wandering Negress, playing the mandolin, with her jar beside her (vase containing drinking water) sleeps deeply, worn out by fatigue. A lion wanders by, detects her and doesn't devour her. There's an effect of moonlight, very poetic. The scene takes place in a completely arid desert. The Gypsy is dressed in Oriental fashion."

The mayor of Laval referred the matter to the local museum; Rousseau's offer was never accepted, however, the authorities evidently finding his work as little to their liking as did those who saw the paintings that he regularly submitted to the Salon. The public in general regarded him as a laughing-stock, but a few perceptive critics and artists of the time (Gauguin among them) and, somewhat later, the Cubist painters and poets, admired his art. Subsequently, the Surrealists discovered in his paintings the qualities of naïveté, simplified form, and imaginative power that they particularly valued.

After having been lost to sight for some twenty years, *The Sleeping Gypsy* was rediscovered in the 'twenties. Picasso brought it to the attention of the adviser of the American collector John Quinn, who bought it. When the picture came up for auction after Quinn's death, the Surrealist poet Jean Cocteau wrote a panegyric of it in the catalogue, in which he said: "We have here the contrary of poetic painting, of anecdote. One is confronted, rather, by painted poetry, by a poetic object." Pointing out that, in spite of Rousseau's careful attention to detail, there are no footprints on the sands around the gypsy's feet, Cocteau suggested that the lion and the river may be the dream of the sleeper.

Scorned by the public of its day, and first esteemed by artists and poets, *The Sleeping Gypsy* is now one of the most popular paintings in The Museum of Modern Art.

HILAIRE-GERMAIN-EDGAR DEGAS. French, 1834–1917. *At the Milliner's.* c. 1882. Pastel, 27⅝ x 27¾ inches. Gift of Mrs. David M. Levy. [141.57]

Though *At the Milliner's* is the earliest in date of the paintings in this book, and indeed one of the earliest in The Museum of Modern Art, at the time it was done it epitomized modernity. Its modernism lay in its touches of pure color, with the high-keyed tones favored by the Impressionists contrasting with darker areas; the choice of a contemporary, even trivial, subject; and, especially, the daring composition with uptilted perspective and figures cut by the framing edges. We view the scene as if in a snapshot; but, although Degas was in fact interested in photography, it was probably also a growing familiarity with Japanese prints, then much appreciated in Paris, that led him and other artists of the time to adopt the seemingly casual composition of their pictures, as well as a high vantage point that contradicts the traditional Western scheme of deep perspective, in which lines converge toward a single vanishing point.

Degas once defined the abiding principle of art as "the summing up of life in its essential gestures." His interest in occupational attitudes led to his many studies of ballet dancers, women bathing, and laundresses washing or ironing. *At the Milliner's* is one of more than a dozen works that he made at about this date with a millinery shop as the subject. Here, he has caught in one vivid glimpse both the pleased expression and the gesture of the woman trying on a bonnet, as well as the action of the attendant proffering two others for her approval. The picture is rendered in pastel, a medium Degas made particularly his own. He preferred its mat surface to the gloss of oil pigments and liked the freedom it gave him to draw rapidly in color, using broken lines to convey the blurred effect of figures seen in action.

The model for the woman trying on the hat was the American painter Mary Cassatt, who lived and worked in France as a close associate of the Impressionists. She was in large part responsible for stimulating interest in their art in the United States and encouraging patrons in this country to buy their works.

PAUL GAUGUIN. French, 1848–1903. In Tahiti and the Marquesas, 1891–1893, 1895–1903. *Still Life with Three Puppies*. 1888. Oil on wood, 36⅛ x 24⅝ inches. Mrs. Simon Guggenheim Fund. [48.52]

The *Still Life with Three Puppies* was painted only a few years after Degas' *At the Milliner's* and likewise shows the influence of Japanese prints in its uptilted perspective and flattened space. In every other respect, however, this picture reveals how radically Gauguin had broken with the premise of the Impressionists, with whom he had until recently been associated. Whereas they sought to capture in their paintings a fleeting moment of life and show it with utmost fidelity, Gauguin asserted that "painting is an abstraction." He demonstrated his dictum by constructing compositions that were deliberately artificial in their choice of color, dark-and-light contrasts, and spatial arrangement of simplified forms drawn with accentuated outlines and a wholly arbitrary use of cast shadows.

Alfred H. Barr, Jr. has pointed out: "As in the fairy tale of *Goldilocks and the Three Bears* the objects in this still life . . . come by threes—three puppies, three blue goblets, three apples." Gauguin found inspiration for creating an art of intentionally childlike simplicity in the illustrations of children's books and the peasant art of Brittany, where he painted the *Still Life with Three Puppies*. Paradoxically enough, however, the still-life-within-a-still-life in the lower right corner is a testimony to his continuing admiration for Cézanne, one of whose canvases of fruit on a table cloth (somewhat similar to that reproduced on page 30) he owned and took with him to Brittany.

Two years after painting this picture, Gauguin set off for the South Seas, in quest of an environment still more primitive and remote from European conventions.

15

VINCENT VAN GOGH. Dutch, 1853–1890. In France from 1886. *The Starry Night.* 1889. Oil on canvas, 29 x 36¼ inches. Acquired through the Lillie P. Bliss Bequest. [472.41]

To Vincent van Gogh, coming to Provence in 1888 from his native Netherlands and a two-year sojourn in Paris, the brilliant sunlight and vivid colors of the Midi were intoxicating. Even though this is a night scene, it is pervaded with a southern intensity of blues, greens, and yellows. The moon is as burningly radiant as the sun; the stars explode like fireworks.

Soon after his arrival in Arles, van Gogh wrote of wanting to create a "star-spangled sky," and in subsequent letters he noted that this idea continued to haunt him. *The Starry Night* is the second and more visionary of his two versions of the theme. Above the rooftops of the quiet village, the curves of the surrounding hills are first paralleled and then exaggerated by the turbulence in the sky, which rolls onward like a roaring ocean. The left-to-right motion across the canvas is punctuated by two vertical accents: the cypress trees at the left, soaring upward like flames, and the pointed spire of the church in the middle distance. Swirling strokes of thickly laid-on pigment enhance the rhythmic effect and express the fervent emotion underlying van Gogh's nocturnal vision.

GEORGES-PIERRE SEURAT. French, 1859–1891. *Port-en-Bessin, Entrance to the Harbor.* 1888. Oil on canvas, 21⅝ x 25⅝ inches. Lillie P. Bliss Collection. [126.34]

Although painted just a year before van Gogh's *Starry Night,* Seurat's *Port-en-Bessin* could hardly present a greater contrast. Instead of a Provençal landscape, which even at night seems to retain the brilliance of a sun-drenched day, we have the pale and hazy atmosphere along the Normandy seacoast. In place of van Gogh's agitated sky, here the serenity overhead is reflected in the tranquil water, upon which the shadows cast by the clouds form five symmetrically placed ovals. The central one provides a backdrop for the two overlapping fishing boats placed almost precisely midway between the sides of the canvas.

"Calm of line," Seurat wrote, "is given by the horizontal." In the *Port-en-Bessin,* horizontals prevail. They lead backward from the gentle curve of the pathway in the foreground to the breakwaters in the middle distance and, finally, to the unbroken line of the high, distant horizon. The only vertical accents are those provided by the masts and pointed sails of the fleet.

Seurat's painting technique, also, could hardly differ more from the vigorous impetuosity of van Gogh's thick brushstrokes. Here, each dot of pigment has been separately placed, its position methodically calculated with respect to those around it. Seurat had closely studied the color theories of nineteenth-century physicists and, seeking to attain purity of tone and clarity of light, painstakingly used the tip of his brush to juxtapose minute dots of color, intermixed with white. Seen at a little distance, these points blend to produce an effect of shimmering luminosity. With equal precision, Seurat painted a dotted frame to enclose the seascape's overall blondness within a darker tonality.

HENRI DE TOULOUSE-LAUTREC. French, 1864–1901. *La Goulue at the Moulin Rouge*. 1891–1892. Oil on cardboard, 31¼ x 23¼ inches. Gift of Mrs. David M. Levy. [161.57]

The Moulin Rouge, which opened in Montmartre in 1889, quickly became the most popular of the *café concerts* that were a distinguishing feature of Paris night life toward the close of the last century. Here artists, entertainers, intellectuals, and people of every social class foregathered to dance, gossip, and see the cabaret show, which drew on the varied talents of singers, dancers, clowns, and contortionists; and here Toulouse-Lautrec loved to go, not only for diversion but also to sketch the ever-changing spectacle offered by the habitués.

La Goulue ("the Glutton") was the nickname of Louise Weber, who was the reigning belle of this milieu

for a brief time, until her voracious appetite caused her to become grossly fat. Toulouse-Lautrec has shown her at the height of her favor as, arrogant and self-assured, she enters arm in arm with two companions. Their sober, high-necked costumes serve as foils to her light, filmy dress, with its deeply plunging décolletage accentuated by a sprig of green and the demure black ribbon encircling her neck. The types of the three women, too, are artfully contrasted. The wasp-waisted figure of the still-slender dancer is set off by the plumpness of the woman at the left, while the piquant profile of the pretty young girl at the right makes one all the more conscious of the pinched mouth and hardened expression of La Goulue, whose face beneath its heavy makeup already shows the ravages of age and dissipation.

Again, as in Degas' *At the Milliner's* (page 14), the figures are cut off by the edges of the picture. The space here is even shallower, and the three principal figures are brought forward to the front plane. The flattened shapes, patterning of dark-and-light contrasts, and rhythmic curves are all devices that Toulouse-Lautrec used to great effect in his posters.

KEES VAN DONGEN. French, born the Netherlands. 1877–1968. To France 1897. *Modjesko, Soprano Singer.* 1908. Oil on canvas, 39⅜ x 32 inches. Gift of Mr. and Mrs. Peter A. Rübel. [192.55]

The *café concert* remained popular well into the twentieth century. In this painting, made almost two decades after Toulouse-Lautrec's *La Goulue at the Moulin Rouge,* van Dongen has given us the portrait of another cabaret entertainer, a well-known female impersonator. The clashing violence of the colors—unnaturally yellow flesh and dark blue hair topped by a pink and green headdress, with bright red surrounding the figure and isolating it from the pink and mauve background—suggests the strident voice issuing from the heavily rouged lips.

The single figure against its flat background is far more like a poster than is Toulouse-Lautrec's *La Goulue.* In fact, when the *Modjesko, Soprano Singer* was first shown in a large exhibition of van Dongen's work, in the year that it was painted, the critic Marius-Ary Leblond remarked in the foreword to the catalogue: "Here, the painting condenses the poster into art; the person is himself a poster, shrieking in red. [It] offers a new type of art, close to the poster but superior to it, tasteful in another way, presenting the soft sensuousness of paint with a spicy freshness—an art of phantasmagoric virtuosity."

JAMES ENSOR. Belgian, 1860-1949. *Masks Confronting Death.* 1888. Oil on canvas, 32 x 39½ inches. Mrs. Simon Guggenheim Fund. [505.51]

On the ground floor of the house in Ostend where Ensor was born, his mother's family kept a souvenir shop, where sea shells, porcelain, fans, chinoiserie, puppets, and masks were sold. The masks were of particular importance because the mid-Lenten carnival was elaborately celebrated in Ostend. Images of the carnival, during which bands of figures in fancy dress thronged the streets and reality was cloaked and distorted by fantasy, mingle in Ensor's art with images of death, which became increasingly frequent in his work after his father died in 1887. In the *Masks Confronting Death,* there may also be a reminiscence of such late-medieval allegorical representations as the Triumph of Death, which shows a gay band of courtiers out hunting, who suddenly encounter corpses in various stages of decomposition; or the Dance of Death, which portrays the skeleton as the ultimate guise of every mortal, be he emperor or beggar.

In this painting, Ensor has exploited to the full the expressionist possibilities inherent in the exaggerated features of carnival masks. "Scandalized, insolent, cruel, malicious masks," he wrote. "I have joyfully shut myself in the solitary milieu ruled by the mask with a face of violence and brilliance. And the mask cried to me: Freshness of tone, sharp expression, sumptuous decor, great unexpected gestures, unplanned movements, exquisite turbulence." The emotional impact of the *Masks Confronting Death* is all the greater because it is not painted in somber, funereal tones but in vivid, high-keyed colors drenched with light—which Ensor called "the Queen of our senses."

PAUL KLEE. German, 1879–1940. Born and died in Switzerland. *Actor's Mask.* 1924. Oil on canvas mounted on board, 14½ x 13⅜ inches. The Sidney and Harriet Janis Collection. [616.67]

In his formative years, Klee was influenced by Ensor, and perhaps this may first have attracted him to the theme of masks. The theater, however, was always among the most constant of Klee's interests, recurring hundreds of times as a subject in his art. He frequented theatrical and ethnographical museums, and during the 'twenties made for his son a Punch-and-Judy show peopled with numerous puppets, many of them revealing his familiarity with primitive masks and sculpture. Physiognomy is another dominant theme throughout Klee's art. In many of his works, he reveals the close connection between humans and animals, and even their interchangeability—a con-

cept often encountered in primitive cultures and children's fairy tales, as well as in Ensor's carnival figures.

In the *Actor's Mask,* on the other hand, the face despite its catlike eyes bears less resemblance to an animal than to some geological formation. The frontal image with its hypnotic stare is almost completely flattened, so that here, as the critic Andrew Forge has noted, "mask and face are one." He goes on to say: "The strata-like formation out of which the features grow is ancient. It is as though time had slowly pressed out the eyes, the mouth. Pressure seems to bear across the face in the parallel red lines. The yellow features, with their gathering of red lines, suggest a bursting through of the surface by an even greater pressure." The hair is rendered with the same system of striations that Klee sometimes used, at about the same date as this painting, for landscapes or botanical subjects.

EMIL NOLDE (Emil Hansen). Danish, born North Schleswig, Germany (later part of Denmark). 1867–1956. Worked in Germany. *Christ among the Children.* 1910. Oil on canvas, 34⅛ x 41⅞ inches. Gift of Dr. W. R. Valentiner. [341.55]

A number of twentieth-century artists have been as stirred as were the old masters by the drama and human appeal, as well as the spirituality, of biblical episodes. As a rule, however, they have not adhered to traditional iconography but have sought new ways in which to interpret the familiar religious themes. This is true of Nolde, although his *Christ among the Children* is a quite literal rendering of the passage in the Gospel according to St. Luke (18:15–16) which relates how Christ, rebuking His disciples for attempting to keep away from Him the throngs who pressed about Him with their infants, said, "Suffer little children to come unto me, and forbid them not: for of such is the kingdom of God."

The looseness with which the paint is applied is typical of Nolde. He believed spontaneity to be indispensable for creativity, asserting that "the quicker a painting is done, the better it is." Like many expressionists, he particularly valued the emotive power of color. In this picture, color also assumes a symbolic quality. At the left are the disciples, with swarthy, bearded countenances and somber clothing. In the center, Christ, clad in a mantle of medium blue, bends lovingly toward the right to embrace the eager children, whose radiant joy is denoted by glowing reds and yellows, with touches of bright green.

GEORGES ROUAULT. French, 1871–1958. *Christ Mocked by Soldiers.* 1932. Oil on canvas, $36\frac{1}{4}$ x $28\frac{1}{2}$ inches. Anonymous gift. [414.41]

Nolde's painting portrays a joyous moment in Christ's life; in the *Christ Mocked by Soldiers,* He is shown as the Man of Sorrows. Rouault was a deeply devout man; but though religious subjects constitute a large proportion of his paintings and prints, he often departed from conventional treatment of those themes.

In earlier representations of the Mocking of Christ, He is generally shown being struck or spat upon. Rouault depicts a psychological situation rather than a specific action. The tormentors are not engaged in physical abuse but are characterized as coarse buffoons—dull of under-standing, rather than malevolent; and Christ's bent head and downcast eyes seem to indicate that He is mournfully contemplating the rejection of His message.

In his youth, Rouault had been apprenticed to a stained-glass maker. His predilection for glowing reds and blues, and his use of heavy, dark contours that resemble the leading in medieval church windows, may reflect this early training. Here, the thick black outlines, in combination with the stiff, angular position of Christ's arms, create a sense of rigid tension that is just the opposite of Nolde's relaxed, open forms. Whereas Nolde applied his pigment in broad, fluent washes, Rouault laid on his relatively dry colors in successive layers that allow the underpainting to show through and result in an encrusted surface.

CLAUDE MONET. French, 1840–1926. *Water Lilies.* c. 1920. Oil on canvas; 2 panels of a triptych, each section 6 feet 6 inches x 14 feet. Mrs. Simon Guggenheim Fund. [666.59.1-2]

These panels, the left and central sections of a three-part painting in the Museum's collection, are among a large number of huge canvases portraying Monet's water garden in Giverny, a village on the Seine between Paris and Rouen. Beginning in 1899, Monet painted several series of works on this subject, which, he declared, had become an obsession with him. In 1914, though he was then seventy-four years old and troubled by failing eyesight, he embarked on the project of developing the theme into a great cycle of water landscapes, to fulfil a commission from the government obtained for him by his friend and neighbor, the statesman Georges Clemenceau.

In keeping with the tenets of Impressionism (whose name, in fact, derived from a painting called *Impression—Sunrise,* which he submitted to the first group exhibition arranged by artists of that movement in 1874), Monet's avowed intention was to capture reality with utmost fidelity. He sought to render every nuance of the water, with its flowers, lily pads, and reflections of surrounding trees and overarching sky, as it appeared under the changing conditions of light and atmosphere caused

by weather, season, or time of day. Yet ironically, as Alfred H. Barr, Jr. has written: "The floating, ambiguous images and the flat, steeply rising perspective tend to give the scene an unreal or abstract effect. At the same time, Monet has given emphatic reality to the painted surface by means of broad, sweeping brushstrokes combined with a many-layered, scraped, and scumbled technique of extraordinary richness."

In 1927, the year after Monet's death, nineteen of the panels were installed in the Orangerie, a branch of the Louvre at the end of the Tuileries Gardens in Paris. Others remained all but forgotten in Monet's abandoned studio at Giverny until they were rediscovered in the 'fifties. The garden and water-lily pond were then restored and declared a national monument; and in 1966, on the death of Monet's son, some sixty of the paintings were bequeathed to the Musée Marmottan in Paris.

With this triptych and another related single panel, The Museum of Modern Art is fortunate in possessing the largest group of the series outside France. Here, in the heart of bustling midtown Manhattan, so remote from Monet's peaceful village, the *Water Lilies* fulfils his wish to offer "the illusion of an endless whole, of water without horizon or bank; nerves tense from work would be relaxed there . . . the refuge of a peaceable meditation in the center of a flowering aquarium."

25

EDOUARD VUILLARD. French, 1868–1940. *Mother and Sister of the Artist.* c. 1893. Oil on canvas, 18¼ x 22¼ inches. Gift of Mrs. Saidie A. May. [141.34]

In keeping with Vuillard's adherence to principles formulated a generation earlier by the critic Edmond Duranty, this little picture is both a double portrait of his mother and his sister Marie, and a painting of an interior. An artist, Duranty said, should devote himself to contemporary life, and he should show people casually, as they are, in the midst of their everyday environment, which in fact is an expression of their character.

Vuillard often painted his own milieu, and one of his favorite subjects was his mother, who, widowed while her children were still quite young, supported the family by setting up a dressmaking establishment in her home. Here, instead of showing her at work, as he frequently did, Vuillard has portrayed her seated as if to receive a visitor, to whom Marie, pressed up against the wall, is bowing shyly in greeting. Only a corner of the room is seen, the table at the right and the picture on the left wall being cut off at an angle, in the manner of Degas (see page 14). As Duranty had pointed out: "We are not always standing in the middle of a room, with its walls running neatly away on either side of us. . . . There is in the foreground an expanding space which . . . can lose the ceiling, it can pick up objects on the floor, it can cut off furniture at unexpected angles. Our line of sight is cut off at each side, as if by a frame, and whatever is sliced off by that frame is invisible to us."

The frontal figure of Mme Vuillard in her black dress is set off against the plain surfaces of the floor boards and chest of drawers behind her. She seems indomitable and self-assured, in contrast to the deferential young Marie, whose figure, despite the bold plaid of her dress, merges with the allover pattern of the wallpaper, emphasizing the self-effacement expressed in her attitude. The small size of the picture is well suited to its intimate character.

PIERRE BONNARD. French, 1867–1947. *The Breakfast
Room.* c. 1930–1931. Oil on canvas, 62⅞ x 44⅞ inches.
Anonymous gift. [392.41]

In his youth Bonnard, like Vuillard, belonged to an
avant-garde group that, under the influence of Gauguin,
worked in reaction to Impressionism. Subsequently, he
turned aside from all prevailing modernist tendencies,
electing instead to explore and carry further the Impressionists' legacy of concentration on color and light.

The Breakfast Room with its boldly patterned wallpaper is alive with vibrant color. The still life of the laid
table in the foreground in itself provides a dazzling array
of hues, higher in key than those outdoors as viewed
through the window. Purely naturalistic, local color is
modified or abandoned for the sake of a more arbitrary,
decorative scheme, as evidenced by the blue and purple
shadows cast by the objects on the tablecloth and the
tonality of the window uprights. Pigment is laid on in

short, broken brushstrokes that capture the shimmer of
ever-changing light.

Bonnard differed from the Impressionists in constructing his pictures according to strict rules of balance.
The composition of *The Breakfast Room* is symmetrical.
The vertical lines and planes of the walls, the uprights of
the windows, and the abruptly curtailed figures at the
sides are countered by the horizontals of the far edge of
the table, the lower part of the window sash, and the top
of the balustrade. The diagonal stripes of the tablecloth
lead the eye up and out to the view of the terrace and the
garden beyond. A screen of trees prevents this prospect
from opening out into an unlimited vista; as in Vuillard's
painting (opposite), what we see is a glimpse of a private,
intimate world.

27

PAUL CÉZANNE. French, 1839–1906. *The Bather*. c. 1885. Oil on canvas, 50 x 38⅛ inches. Lillie P. Bliss Collection. [1.34]

Although based upon a photograph of a nude model, the male body in Cézanne's *Bather* is as far removed from photographic realism as it is from classical idealism. From the standpoint of academic "correctness," the drawing is awkward and imprecise, yet the figure rises before us in impressive monumentality. He is not engaged in bathing nor, indeed, in any overt action, but seems to pause in his advancing stride as if lost in meditation or struck by something on the ground before him. The effect of immobility is enhanced by his placement in the center of the canvas and the symmetrical pose of his bent arms, with fingers firmly buttressing the waist. Though the bather's position in the front plane of the picture brings him close to us physically, his bowed head and contemplative, downward gaze make him psychologically remote.

Figure and landscape are interlocked in a system of similarities and contrasts. The repeated horizontals of the background, echoed in the banded lines of the bather's trunks and the fingers above them, serve as counterpoint to his vertical form. The flesh of his body is the same color as the stretch of ground behind him; its blue and violet shadows and rosy highlights are like the tones of the rocks, water, and sky. The same type of brushwork is used for both figure and landscape. It is a complex juxtaposition of strokes, which neither suggest texture nor model form in a conventional way but which, through their freely changing character, impart a sense of vibrancy to the surface of the canvas. They make us constantly aware that what we are looking at is not a simulacrum of the visible world but is instead an artificial construct—a painting.

Equally important in this respect is the manner of drawing, with lines that are sometimes long, continuous curves and elsewhere broken and angular. Instead of delineating the contours of the body, they obey their own rhythmic, seemingly arbitrary laws. The dark half-oval line at the bottom of the bather's face, for example, does not correspond to the structure of his chin; and immediately to the left, there is a break before the beginning of the dark strokes defining his right shoulder and upper arm. Here again, the strokes do not bound these parts of his body but suggest the existence of other planes that might be revealed if he were to shift position. They also imply that the spectator's gaze, too, is constantly shifting. Thus, the lack of motion in the subject portrayed is counteracted by the freedom and variation of the lines and brushwork. Instead of freezing his image within a moment of time, Cézanne leads the viewer to an ongoing visual exploration, somewhat analogous to his own process of observation and re-creation in the course of painting the picture.

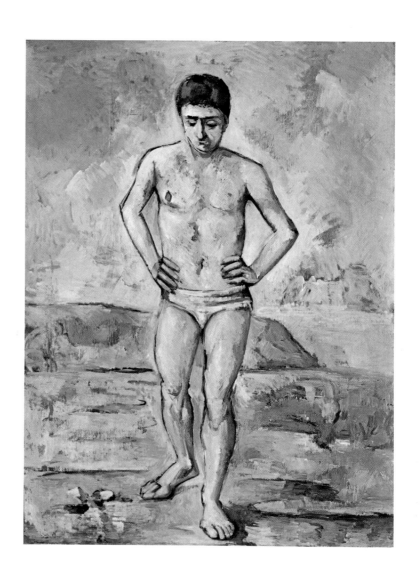

PAUL CÉZANNE. French, 1839–1906. *Still Life with Apples.* 1895–1898. Oil on canvas, 27 x 36 ½ inches. Lillie P. Bliss Collection. [22.34]

The still life provided Cézanne with a subject ideally suited to his analytical, contemplative manner of working. To obtain contrasts of color and form, he could choose and arrange objects, which would remain immobile under his protracted scrutiny. In this unfinished painting, a lemon, apples, and a glass are placed upon a rumpled white napkin thrown over an underlying tablecloth. Behind them stand a compotier and a figured jug, and at the left are folds of a patterned drapery.

Cézanne took from the Impressionists, with whom he was briefly associated, the practice of painting directly from nature with small touches of pure, luminous color. But whereas the Impressionists tried to capture momentary effects and preferred high-keyed tones that made objects appear to dissolve in a shimmer of light and atmosphere, Cézanne sought instead to emphasize the solidity and basic geometric structure of his forms, and to create a sense of permanence rather than transience.

To achieve his aim, he closely observed the manner in which local colors appear altered by the recession of planes and the reflection of adjacent objects. These modulations he translated by small, elongated strokes into a system of tonal gradations. Intensely concentrated observation of his motif was followed by painstaking selection of the colors that would best render each nuance and enable him, in his own phrase, to "realize his sensations before nature," confident that "when the color has its appropriate richness, the form will attain its full volume."

The *Still Life with Apples,* like the earlier *Bather* (page 29), shows Cézanne's subtle distortions of nature. The table top is uptilted, and outlines are discontinuous to indicate the existence of multiple planes shifting in depth. As in *The Bather,* the handling of the brushstrokes makes us realize that we are not looking at a literal representation of nature but at a painting that reconstructs the artist's response to it. This, however, is not the intensely subjective response of an expressionist such as van Gogh, for example, whose *Starry Night* (page 16) makes us as aware of his own emotion as of the scene he portrays. While fully conscious of the voluptuous appeal of his motif, Cézanne's approach is more objective. He externalizes his sensations, analyzes what produces them, and concentrates on the problems of transcribing them. He offers both an intellectual and a sensuous experience.

PAUL CÉZANNE. *Pines and Rocks* (Fontainebleau?). 1896–1899. Oil on canvas, 32 x 25¾ inches. Lillie P. Bliss Collection. [16.34]

This painting was formerly dated about 1904 and thought to have been painted in or around Aix, where Cézanne spent the final years of his life. More recently, it has been assigned to a somewhat earlier period, on the basis of the thinness with which the paint is applied and the rather small, often diagonally slanted brushstrokes. It has also been suggested that the locale represented is not in Provence but rather in the north—either in the Forest of Fontainebleau or some other region near Paris, where Cézanne spent a good deal of time in the late 'nineties.

If the *Pines and Rocks* recalls some of the evanescent, fitful light of Impressionism, its composition is firmly structured by the repeated verticals of the slender, upward-soaring tree trunks and the contrasting slanting faces of the massive rocks. At first glance, the range of color seems a limited one—all blues, greens, and browns. The blue tonality that pervades the canvas denotes both sky and atmosphere. The green patches on the ground below are echoed in the foliage above. It is only as one looks more closely that the innumerable variations of shades become apparent, as well as the violets, yellows, and reds. In contrast to the use of Cézanne's characteristic system of parallel strokes in some areas, elsewhere the colors blend into one another, and the paint seems to have been applied as loosely and rapidly as in a watercolor, creating a sense of airiness and light.

31

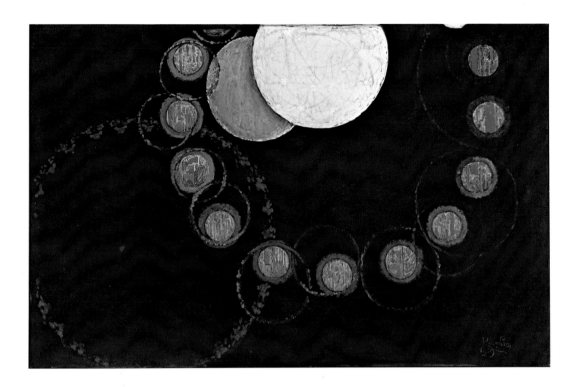

František Kupka. Czech, 1871–1957. In France from 1895. *The First Step.* 1910–1913? (dated on painting 1909). Oil on canvas, 32¾ x 51 inches. Hillman Periodicals Fund. [562.56]

The paintings reproduced on this and the opposite page—one dark, the other light—have in common that both are primarily concerned with color, both have astronomical references, and both represent milestones in the development of abstract painting. Both also take as their point of departure Seurat's theories of color contrast (see page 17) and researches by nineteenth-century physicists, ultimately derived from Sir Isaac Newton's analyses of color and light.

Kupka, a highly original and rather solitary artist, began his development toward abstraction about 1909. He was especially interested in how colors, particularly red and blue, are perceived by the viewer. This picture, inspired by an astronomical diagram, shows two large planets surrounded by a ring of moons; but the manner of rendering them makes the work seem to be virtually an abstract painting—perhaps the first.

In 1912, Kupka painted a vertical panel called *Disks of Newton* and a large, square canvas called *Fugue in Two Colors.* The musical title of the latter may be explained by a statement that he made to a newspaper correspondent the following year: "Music is an art of sounds that are not in nature and almost entirely created. Man created writings, the airplane, and the locomotive. Why may he not create in painting independently of the forms and colors of the world about him? . . . I believe I can produce a fugue in colors as Bach has done in music." Many years later, he gave the Museum's painting its title, indicating that he considered it the "first step" toward the *Fugue.*

ROBERT DELAUNAY. French, 1885–1941. *Simultaneous Contrasts: Sun and Moon.* 1913 (dated on painting 1912). Oil on canvas, 53 inches diameter. Mrs. Simon Guggenheim Fund. [1.54]

This painting belongs to a series, done about 1912–1913, to which Delaunay gave the generic name Simultaneous Contrasts. He took the term from a book, *On the Law of the Simultaneous Contrast of Colors,* published in 1839 by the physicist Michel-Eugène Chevreul, whose theories also influenced Seurat and his followers, as well as Kupka. The basic concept, which Delaunay adopted as an aesthetic principle, was that certain colors change one another's aspect when the beholder observes them at the same time. Like Kupka, Delaunay explained his art by musical analogies, saying that he "played with colors as one may express oneself in music, by a fugue of colored, fugued phrases."

In this picture, as in several other paintings by Delaunay of this period, the sun and moon provide the point of departure for what is essentially a purely abstract painting. Delaunay declared that he had decided to abandon all "images of reality that come to corrupt the order of color." Eliminating chiaroscuro, perspective, and effects of volume, in this work he relies solely for his expressive means on contrasts of color and the rhythmic interplay between the circular canvas and the overlapping circles and ovals within it. "The breaking up of form by light creates colored planes," Delaunay said. "These colored planes are the structure of the picture, and nature is no longer a subject for description but a pretext."

33

Josef Albers. American, born Germany. 1888–1976. To U.S.A. 1933. *Homage to the Square: Broad Call.* 1967. Oil on composition board, 48 x 48 inches. The Sidney and Harriet Janis Collection. [664.67]

Many modern artists have devoted themselves to the problem of the interaction of color explored by Kupka and Delaunay (pages 32 and 33), but none has done so with greater tenacity than Albers. His Homage to the Square series, begun in 1949, was carried on up to the time of his death. Though each work consists of a symmetrical arrangement of squares-within-squares, they differ from one another in the placement and proportion of these elements and the choice of colors, attaining a strikingly rich variety.

As a man-made, universal symbol, the square was selected by Albers to become "the stage, the actor and the voice which perform the endless drama of the excite-

ments of color instrumentation." He applied his paint directly from the tube, generally with a palette knife, and laid it on as thinly and evenly as possible, allowing no textural effects to interfere with the autonomy of the colors and their free interplay.

A meticulous craftsman, Albers customarily inscribed on the back of each of his works a list of the pigments used and the names of their manufacturers. For the *Homage to the Square: Broad Call,* he employed four kinds of red oil paints. He has explained that, nevertheless, its color instrumentation may be read in three colors: "The central red and the outer appear touching each other underneath a third translucent red which overlaps the 2 first ones within 2 illusionary frames of equal width. Then the third red, acting as an intermediary color, turns the darker underneath—lighter, and the lighter underneath—deeper, although all colors used are fully opaque."

MARK ROTHKO. American, born Latvia. 1903–1970. To U.S.A. 1913. *Red, Brown, and Black.* 1958. Oil on canvas, 8 feet 10⅝ inches x 9 feet 9¼ inches. Mrs. Simon Guggenheim Fund. [21.59]

Rothko's paintings from the late 'forties on have in common with those of Albers their concentration upon color and their dependence upon a simple geometrical shape—in Rothko's case, the rectangle rather than the square. Here, however, the similarity ends. In place of the sharp precision of Albers' squares, Rothko's rectangles are blurred, with irregular edges. This gives them a three-dimensional effect, though they seem less like solid bodies than impalpable clouds capable of expanding within an enveloping atmosphere. Their potentiality for

change is also implied by the subtle modulations within the mat painted surfaces, which become increasingly apparent the longer one gazes at them. This is exactly the opposite of Albers' deliberate suppression of any trace of brushwork or variation in the application of pigment.

The *Red, Brown, and Black* is in the dark, somber tonality that Rothko favored toward the end of his life. The large size of the work, characteristic of many postwar paintings by American abstractionists (such as those shown on pages 139–44), is essential for its powerful impact. Rothko's suspended rectangles, floating close to the front plane of the canvas, loom up imposingly before the spectator. As he once remarked, "My paintings are sometimes described as façades, and indeed, they are façades."

KASIMIR MALEVICH. Russian, 1878–1935. *Suprematist Composition: Red Square and Black Square.* 1914 or 1915? Oil on canvas, 28 x 17½ inches. [816.35]

A year or so after Delaunay, in Paris, had completed the *Sun and Moon* (page 33), Malevich, in Moscow, working with simple geometrical figures, took an even more decisive step toward ridding art of any reference to the natural world. Beginning with nothing but a black square drawn in lead pencil on a white ground, Malevich went on to produce a number of totally abstract works. The *Red Square and Black Square* is one of a series of thirty-five Suprematist Compositions that he exhibited in 1915.

Some were even simpler than this—a black square on a white ground; a circle; and two identical, symmetrically placed squares.

In this painting, the black square has been placed off center, and the smaller square tilted on its axis and painted red. In others of the series, rectangles and even trapezoids were introduced, the colors included blue and green as well as black and red, the number of elements was increased, and the relationships among them became progressively more complex and dynamic. Of the basic shape used here, Malevich declared: "The square is not a subconscious form. It is the creation of intuitive reason. It is the face of the new art. The square is a living, royal infant. It is the first step of pure creation in art."

Malevich called his art Suprematism, to signify "the supremacy of pure feeling or perception in the pictorial arts." He explained its premises in 1916: "The artist can be a creator only when the forms in his picture have nothing in common with nature. . . . Forms must be given life and the right to individual existence."

The Suprematist Compositions of Malevich and his followers were the first purely geometrical abstractions, opening up a pathway that artists have continued to explore ever since. Malevich, however, did not use the term "abstract" for such works but called them "non-objective," to indicate their complete liberation from representation; and he proclaimed Suprematism "the new realism in painting."

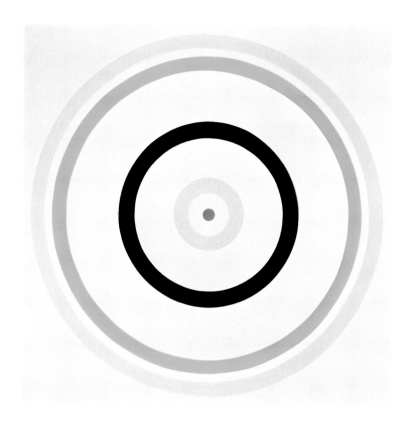

KENNETH NOLAND. American, born 1924. *Turnsole*. 1961. Synthetic polymer paint on canvas, 7 feet 10 ¼ inches x 7 feet 10¼ inches. Blanchette Rockefeller Fund. [5.68]

Artists who choose to restrict themselves to such simple geometrical shapes as squares or circles accomplish more than a negative purging from their art of references to the natural world. By reducing their expressive means, they force themselves, and those who look at their works, to concentrate on such essentials as the relationship between the size and shape of the canvas, and the forms painted upon it; the relationship between these forms and the ground against which they are placed; the spaces between the forms; and the interaction of the colors.

Noland's *Turnsole* may be regarded as a distant descendant, almost half a century later, of Malevich's Suprematist Compositions, and a closer descendant of the Homage to the Square series of Albers (page 34), with whom Noland studied. It differs from these predecessors in several important respects, most notably its large scale.

As we look at this painting, we become aware of several paradoxes. On the one hand, there is its emphasis on flatness, further enhanced by the fact that the pigments are stained directly into the raw canvas. At the same time, the strong difference in value between the light color of some of the rings, the dark blue central disk, and the black of one of the surrounding rings, sets up a pulsation that makes the forms seem alternately to recede and come forward. Secondly, despite its total abstraction, this concentric composition of purely geometrical shapes inevitably evokes associations with other images, such as a target with a bull's-eye or a diagram of the solar system (its title, however, is another name for "sunflower"). Thus, the *Turnsole*, like many modern paintings, though ostensibly straightforward and simple, is far more ambiguous and complex than is immediately apparent, thereby enticing the spectator into more than casual contemplation.

Theo van Doesburg (C. E. M. Küpper). Dutch, 1883–
1931. *Rhythm of a Russian Dance.* 1918. Oil on canvas,
53½ x 24¼ inches. Acquired through the Lillie P. Bliss
Bequest. [135.46]

A few years after Malevich started from scratch to create
a "pure" art from simple geometrical forms, a group of
artists in the Netherlands achieved total abstraction by
working in the opposite direction. They began with
naturalistic forms and, by analyzing their essential elements, gradually reduced—or abstracted—them to compositions constructed entirely of rectilinear shapes.

The *Rhythm of a Russian Dance* is the culmination of
a detailed analysis that van Doesburg carried out through
a sequence of seven preceding studies (also owned by the
Museum). He moved progressively from his first naturalistic sketch of a dancer to the final painting, which is
composed of flat bars arranged at right angles to one another in such a way that their shapes, and the spatial intervals between them, are an abstract transcription of the
rhythmic, staccato dance movements.

Van Doesburg was the organizer and principal theorist
of a group of painters and architects, whom he brought
together in 1917 under the name of *De Stijl* ("the Style").
Their aesthetic principles restricted the artist's means to
the basic minimum of the straight line and right angle
(symbols of man's intellectual dominance over the dif-
fuse, capricious forms of nature) and to the three primary
colors red, yellow, and blue, together with the neutrals
black, gray, and white. They regarded the painting thus
created as the new, universal art of the future and named
it Neo-Plasticism. It was described as "abstract-real
because it stands between the absolute-abstract and the
natural, or concrete-real. It is not as abstract as thought-
abstraction, and not as real as tangible reality. It is essentially living, plastic representation: the visual expression in which each opposite is transformed into the other."

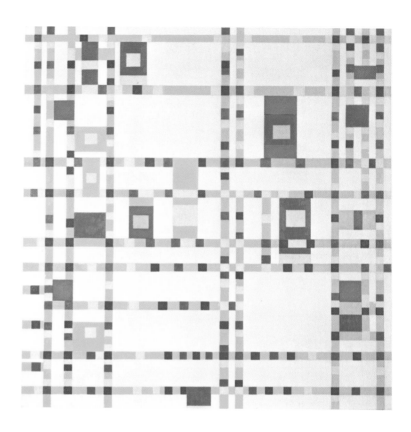

PIET MONDRIAN. Dutch, 1872–1944. Worked in Paris 1912–1914, 1919–1938; in New York 1940–1944. *Broadway Boogie Woogie*. 1942–1943. Oil on canvas, 50 x 50 inches. Anonymous gift. [73.43]

The author of the quotation on the opposite page was Piet Mondrian, a cofounder with van Doesburg of De Stijl. (One of the paintings in his progression from naturalism to pure geometrical abstraction is shown on page 49.) Once having adopted the strict tenets of Neo-Plasticism, Mondrian adhered to them throughout his life, at times producing extremely ascetic compositions of only a few rectangles separated by black bars. The *Broadway Boogie Woogie*, however, is much more complicated. The square and rectangular elements are greatly increased in number and diminished in size, so that the painting is far more agitated than van Doesburg's *Rhythm of a Russian Dance*. Part of its dynamic excitement is due to its asymmetry, and to the manner in which the bands of color

intersect the edges of the unframed canvas. Mondrian was the first to abandon the use of enclosing frames, adopting instead the device of having his paintings project forward from a mount, in order "to move the picture into our surroundings and give it real existence."

Mondrian's *Broadway Boogie Woogie*, his last completed work, was painted in New York, where he came to live during the Second World War, and it reflects the accelerated tempo of the American metropolis. A devotee of dancing and jazz even before coming to this country, Mondrian declared: "True Boogie Woogie I conceive as homogeneous in intention with mine in painting: destruction of melody which is the equivalent of destruction of natural appearance; and construction through the continuous opposition of pure means—dynamic rhythm." The painting was executed with the aid of a technical shortcut that Mondrian learned in America—the use of strips of adhesive tape to lay out his composition on the canvas.

39

Wassily Kandinsky. Russian, 1866–1944. Worked in Germany and France. *Panel 3* and *Panel 4.* 1914. Oil on canvas, 64 x 36¼ inches and 64 x 31½ inches. Mrs. Simon Guggenheim Fund. [2.54 and 3.54]

Diametrically opposed to the orderly construction and restricted color range of the paintings by Malevich, van Doesburg, and Mondrian (pages 36, 38, and 39) are these two panels, from a series of four commissioned for the New York apartment of Edwin R. Campbell. Depicting neither recognizable objects nor geometrical shapes, they evoke the response of our emotion rather than our intellect. Four years earlier, Kandinsky had painted the first purely abstract expressionist picture. Though objects seemed an impediment to his intention of letting the viewer "forget himself and dissolve into the picture," he had difficulty finding forms with which to replace them, since he could never bring himself "to use a form which developed out of the application of logic—not purely from *feeling* within me. . . . All the forms which I have ever used . . . created themselves while I was working, often surprising me."

The panels were separated after Campbell's death in 1929. This pair came to light in the 'fifties and was subsequently identified as complementing two panels in The Solomon R. Guggenheim Museum. It has been suggested that the series may represent the seasons (these being Summer and Spring); but Kandinsky's statement that his paintings are "a graphic representation of a mood and not . . . of objects" should make us wary.

ARSHILE GORKY (Vosdanig Manoog Adoian). American, born Turkish Armenia. 1904–1948. To U.S.A. 1920. *Agony.* 1947. Oil on canvas, 40 x 50½ inches. A. Conger Goodyear Fund. [88.50]

Painted more than thirty years after Kandinsky's panels, Gorky's *Agony* shares with them a reliance on indeterminate forms, lines, and above all, color, to convey an emotional content. But in contrast to the joyousness, buoyancy, and generally high-keyed colors in Kandinsky's *Panel 3* and *Panel 4,* which the black lines and areas serve only to intensify, Gorky's canvas with its darker reds, mauves, browns, pale yellows, and weighty patches of black imparts a sense of tragedy and foreboding. The title *Agony* aptly describes the mood of this work, which was painted in the last year of Gorky's life, during which he suffered a crushing series of misfortunes in his health, personal life, and career.

Kandinsky's forms seem to float in open space; Gorky's are situated within an interior defined by the lines of the floor and a wall in the background. The stage thus constructed is occupied by objects and by hybrid figures, vaguely animate or even humanoid in appearance. They are, however, only metaphors for personages; Gorky declared, "I never put a face on an image."

Whereas Kandinsky created his paintings in bursts of creative ecstasy, Gorky, a consummate draughtsman, made preparatory drawings for his major compositions. The final versions nevertheless generally differ considerably from these studies, for to a great extent they were allowed to develop through free improvisation in the course of execution. Such a procedure had precedents in Kandinsky's spontaneous manner of working and, later, in the theory and practice of the Surrealists, who emphasized the role of automatism and the unconscious as wellsprings of creativity.

41

HENRI MATISSE. French, 1869–1954. *Dance*. 1909. Oil on canvas, 8 feet 6½ inches x 12 feet 9½ inches. Gift of Nelson A. Rockefeller in honor of Alfred H. Barr, Jr. [201.63]

While spending the summer of 1905 on the French coast near the Spanish border, Matisse watched Catalan fishermen dancing in a circle on the beach. He incorporated a ring of dancers into the background of his large canvas *Joy of Life,* which was painted in 1905–1906 and bought by the American collectors Leo and Gertrude Stein. It was seen in their Paris salon by a Russian businessman, Sergei I. Shchukin, who in the dozen years before the First World War was the greatest collector of modern French painting in the world, and he commissioned Matisse to develop the subject of the dance into a mural panel for his palatial house in Moscow.

In this, the first version of the composition Matisse produced in response to the commission, the fishermen have been transformed into female nudes, and the somewhat formal measure of their traditional dance, the sardana, stepped up to a more freely exuberant pace. There are numerous departures from naturalism toward abstraction. Colors are limited to simple areas of green grass, blue sky, and flesh tones, with blacks and browns for the dancers' hair. The bodies have been flattened to silhouettes, without modeling and with only a few lines to indicate features or anatomical details. The rear figures are as large as those in the foreground, eliminating perspective and further flattening the apparent depth within the picture.

After seeing this panel, Shchukin wrote Matisse that he found it of "such nobility, that I am resolved to brave our bourgeois opinion and hang on my staircase a subject with nudes"; and he commissioned a second panel, *Music.* But when he saw the completed works at the Salon of 1910, he demurred, saying that as he had recently adopted two young girls, it might be unseemly to display these nudes so prominently in his house. Two years later, however, Shchukin overcame his scruples, and the final, more intensely violent version of the *Dance,* with its companion piece *Music,* was sent to Moscow. They are now in the Hermitage Museum, Leningrad.

GINO SEVERINI. Italian, 1883–1966. *Dynamic Hieroglyphic of the Bal Tabarin.* 1912. Oil on canvas, with sequins, 63⅝ x 61½ inches. Acquired through the Lillie P. Bliss Bequest. [288.49]

This kaleidoscopic picture packed with details could hardly differ more from the openness and simplifications in Matisse's panel, though the theme of both works is the movement of dancers, presented by means of abstract rhythmic forms. Likewise, though Severini's painting depicts the night life of a Paris café, it is equally far removed from Toulouse-Lautrec's scene at the Moulin Rouge (page 18).

Painted in a small town in Italy on the basis of sketches made in Paris, this "dynamic hieroglyphic" is a synthesis of remembered impressions of actual experience, made up of dislocated fragments recalled in free association. Bits and pieces of identifiable figures and objects—the women's swirling skirts, curls, ruffles, and ribbons; the men's top hats, monocles, white shirt fronts, and ties; the parti-colored pennants used for decoration—are combined with words that further trigger recollections, among them "Polka" and "Valse" to suggest music and dancing. The curves flowing across the canvas are intersected by verticals that splinter the scene like flashes of a stroboscopic light. All sense of depth is annihilated, the rainbow-hued sequins glued onto the canvas serving to emphasize its surface as well as to evoke, together with the bright colors of the paint, the gay and glittering spectacle of the Bal Tabarin.

FRANCIS PICABIA. French, 1879-1953. Active in New York and Barcelona 1913-1917. *I See Again in Memory My Dear Udnie.* 1914 (begun 1913?). Oil on canvas, 8 feet 2½ inches x 6 feet 6¼ inches. Hillman Periodicals Fund. [4.54]

Aboard ship on a voyage to the United States in 1913, Picabia was fascinated by the dancing of a certain Mlle Napierskowska (whose performances were so suggestive that they caused her arrest during her American tour). In the course of that year and the next, he produced a number of large canvases inspired by his recollections of the star dancer, giving one of them the mysterious name *Udnie* that appears again in the title of this picture.

Whatever their basis in actual experience, these impressions have been completely transformed into abstract terms in Picabia's *I See Again in Memory My Dear Udnie.* He explained his paintings of the time by saying that he did not seek to reproduce objects in nature but "to render external an internal state of mind or feeling" by arrangements of line and color that "suggest the equilibrium of static and dynamic qualities." Here, the general effect is monumental, and the rhythms move upward rather slowly instead of evoking swift motion. Within a three-dimensional setting, lit from ambiguously situated sources, some of the shapes look as if they had been carved out by a fretsaw from shallow slabs, while others suggest the nozzles of hoses. In combination, these elements seem to shed their inanimate character and allude to male sexual organs probing receptive female forms. The sensuousness of the painting is augmented by its unusual color harmonies. Pale creamy tones, warmer pinks, smoky reds, and shades of lavender are concentrated in the center and set off by neutral grays, blacks, and browns.

Picabia, together with his friend Marcel Duchamp (page 56), was one of the first to explore the machine as a symbol for human eroticism. In the next few years, the sexual references in his works with machinelike forms were to become far more overt than they are here.

The Rope Dancer Accompanies Herself With Her Shadows

MAN RAY. American, 1890–1976. Lived in Paris. *The Rope Dancer Accompanies Herself with Her Shadows.* 1916. Oil on canvas, 52 inches x 6 feet 1⅜ inches. Gift of G. David Thompson. [33.54]

Though Man Ray's painting, like Picabia's, was inspired by the movements of a dancer, the two works are as different from each other as either is from Matisse's *Dance* (page 42) or Severini's *Dynamic Hieroglyphic of the Bal Tabarin* (page 43), or as any of these four is from the representations of the dance by van Doesburg (page 38) and Mondrian (page 39). Man Ray has created a wholly abstract composition of two-dimensional negative and positive shapes. The large, angular, vertical areas

of color, painted in flat tones of red, green, blue, yellow, and brown laid on with the palette knife, are offset against a gray background. They are linked together by the scalloped line of the tightrope at the top and the curves spinning out like lassos from the tiny figure of the dancer.

Man Ray has explained that he began by making drawings for three positions of a ballet dancer. After enlarging the forms onto different colored papers, he cut them out and destroyed them, retaining only the surrounding pieces as patterns for his large fields of color. He then added the ballet dancer above and the connecting serpentine curves to recall the original idea, which is explained by the title written at the bottom of the picture.

45

PABLO PICASSO. Spanish, 1881–1973. To France 1904. *Les Demoiselles d'Avignon*. 1907. Oil on canvas, 8 feet x 7 feet 8 inches. Acquired through the Lillie P. Bliss Bequest. [333.39]

Many decades have passed since *Les Demoiselles d'Avignon* was painted, yet on first encounter it still retains the power to shock the spectator almost as much as it did its earliest viewers. This certainly cannot be accounted for by any action taking place within it, for the poses are static, and nothing more dramatic is happening than the drawing back of a curtain at the left and the entry of a woman at the right. The impact of the work is due only in part to the impressive size of the canvas and the distorted manner in which the large figures within it are represented, though this becomes acute in the two women at the right.

The painting is charged with a violence that is implicit throughout: in the tension produced by the crowding of the figures into a shallow, compressed, and ambiguous space; by the way their anatomy is drawn, with sharply jutting angles and unmodulated, sicklelike curves (repeated in the still life in the lower center); and by the jagged highlights, especially noticeable in the background in the right half of the picture.

Picasso was twenty-five years old when, in 1906, perhaps impelled by a desire to compete with his older rival Matisse, whose *Joy of Life* had created a sensation at the Salon des Indépendants that year, he decided to concentrate his energies in creating a monumental composition. He developed his ideas through numerous studies made over many months, before beginning to paint the work in the spring of 1907.

The subject was the interior of a brothel; the title was bestowed on the painting many years later, with ironic reference to a notorious house on the Carrer d'Avinyó (Avignon Street) in Barcelona. Originally, the center of the scene was occupied by a sailor holding a wine vessel, and the figure entering at the left was a man (identified by Picasso as a medical student), who in some of the preparatory drawings carries a skull and in others a book. According to a detailed analysis by Leo Steinberg, these two figures make the picture "an allegory of the involved and the uninvolved in confrontation with the indestructible claims of sex." He believes, however, that as the work developed, its subject became not so much a confrontation between participants and nonparticipants, actors and onlookers, but rather between those contained within the picture and ourselves as observers. The sharp jutting angles and abrupt uptilting of the laid table in the center below especially serve to draw us into the scene, for which the woman at the left performs the function of curtain raiser.

As Picasso worked on the canvas, his style underwent as many radical changes as did the composition. The figure at the left, reminiscent of Egyptian or Assyrian sculpture, and the two nudes in the center are painted in light browns and pinks, tinted rather than modeled by shading. The stylization of their features is particularly apparent in their hypnotically staring eyes. The eye of the woman at the left is seen in full face, though her head is shown in profile; conversely, in the two central figures, the noses are drawn in profile within their frontal faces.

The distortions become far more exaggerated in the two darker, aggressive figures at the right. In them, all vestiges of naturalism are abandoned; their dislocated features and the shading by parallel strokes of hatching give their faces the aspect of barbaric masks rather than of human beings. Picasso recalls that he completed these two figures after having painted the rest of the composition, and it is generally believed that they reflect his first exposure to African Negro sculpture. Steinberg suggests that they are also meant to be still stronger personifications of "sheer sexual energy as the image of a life force . . . divested of all accretions of culture."

Many other influences seem to have inspired Picasso in creating this painting. From Cézanne's bather compositions may have come the manner of fusing figures and background within a shallow space, and the use of a contour line that does not correspond to the fixed outline of a form but implies successive views of it (compare, for example, the leg of the figure at the left with the manner of drawing in Cézanne's *Bather*, page 29). Cézanne's still lifes (such as that on page 30) are echoed in the fruit and tablecloth on the tipped-up table at the base of Picasso's canvas. There are also reminiscences of El Greco's skies and draperies, highlighted with flashes like those of an electrical storm; and of certain conventions found in the archaic, pre-Roman sculpture of the Iberian peninsula.

All these disparate elements are combined in a work of expressive intensity. Steinberg considers Picasso's retention of various stylistic modes to have been purposeful: "He challenges far more than traditional focused perspective. . . . Picasso's ultimate challenge is to the notion that the coherence of the art work demands a stylistic consistency among the things represented; that one style must obtain in every part of the canvas. And the shock of the *Demoiselles* resides largely in the frustration of this expectation. In Picasso's farewell to stylistic consistency, the means of rendering and the modes of experiencing become subjectified—open choices, the acts of a personal will." Steinberg also postulates that the *Demoiselles* is not only a sexual metaphor but that, at the same time, by drawing us as spectators into the depicted scene, it becomes a "forced union of dream image and actuality,"

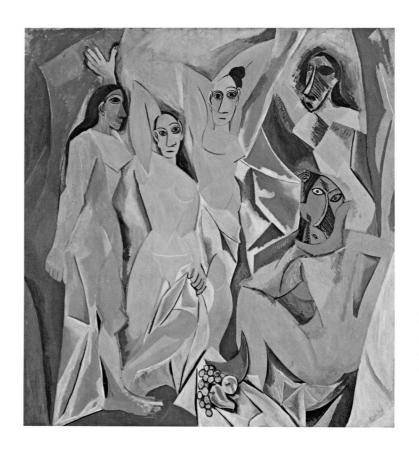

with sexuality being a device "to make visible the immediacy of communion with art. Explosive form and erotic content became reciprocal metaphors for each other."

Whether we accept this interpretation, or any others that have been offered, it is certain that Picasso's painting became widely influential, in spite of the fact that he retained it in his studio without exhibiting it publicly for many years. As Alfred H. Barr, Jr. has pointed out: "*Les Demoiselles d'Avignon* may be called the first cubist pic- ture, for the breaking up of natural forms, whether figures, still life or drapery, into a semi-abstract all-over design of tilting shifting planes compressed into a shallow space is already cubism . . . in a rudimentary stage. . . . *Les Demoiselles* is a transitional picture, a laboratory, a battlefield of trial and experiment"; but, more importantly, over and beyond its historical significance, "it is also a work of formidable, dynamic power, unsurpassed in European art of its time."

PABLO PICASSO. Spanish, 1881–1973. To France 1904. *"Ma Jolie."* 1911–1912. Oil on canvas, 39⅜ x 25¾ inches. Acquired through the Lillie P. Bliss Bequest. [176.45]

In this painting, Picasso carried the process of breaking up natural forms and reconstituting them into a new pictorial reality much further than in *Les Demoiselles d'Avignon* (page 47). The title *"Ma Jolie"* is both the refrain of a popular song of the time and an affectionate reference to Picasso's then-current love. The subject—a woman playing a stringed instrument—is a traditional one; but the lines, planes, shadings, and indications of space are no longer intended, as in conventional paint-ing, to create the illusion of a living personage, and color has been restricted to browns, tans, and grays. Traces of the original theme, such as the outline of the woman's head at the center above, her left arm with bent elbow, the vertical strings of the guitar, the treble clef and stave, and the wine glass at the left, are absorbed within an all-over scaffolding of horizontal and vertical lines. These lines are to be read as the edges of shaded, semitrans-parent planes that indicate diagrammatically the location within a shallow space of parts of the body or objects—not necessarily as they would be seen at one time but with different views and moments combined.

A Cubist painting of this sort, which analyzes elements drawn from perceived reality and reorganizes them into a new composition obedient to its own formal laws, ap-peals to the mind as well as to the eye. The maintaining of recognizable fragments sets up a tension between our perception of a given subject and our mental concept of it, between its illusionistic description and its subordi-nation to an artificially ordered structure.

The letters at the base of the canvas have a double purpose. By emphasizing the surface of the painting, they function together with the clearly distinguishable brush-strokes to serve notice that the "reality" with which we are dealing is that of the picture itself, not that of the "real" world. At the same time, by giving a clue to the underlying theme, they invite us to participate vicarious-ly with the artist in the process of its transformation.

PIET MONDRIAN. Dutch, 1872–1944. Worked in Paris 1912–1914, 1919–1938; in New York 1940–1944. *Composition, V.* 1914. Oil on canvas, 21⅝ x 33⅝ inches. The Sidney and Harriet Janis Collection. [633.67]

In the *Composition, V,* Mondrian went still further than Picasso did in his *"Ma Jolie"* to establish a gridwork of verticals and horizontals as the predominant structure of his painting. Here, the allover pattern of small rectilinear units almost obscures any lingering traces of the original subject. As in a number of Mondrian's paintings of about this date, the theme is a church façade in Paris, but faint references to its arches and the Greek cross of its rose window are all that persists. The composition has been almost completely flattened. There is only a suggestion of atmospheric space in the manner in which the lines of the grid are muffled by light overpainting or fade toward the outer edges. In spite of its greater tendency away from naturalism toward the total geometrical abstraction that Mondrian was to adopt a few years later (see page 39), the *Composition, V* is far less severe in its effect than the *"Ma Jolie."* Paint is brushed on with delicate strokes that blend into one another rather than bluntly asserting their separate identity, and instead of monochromatic tans and grays, there is a soft harmony of pastel blues, pinks, and ochers.

49

JUAN GRIS. (José Victoriano González). Spanish, 1887–1927. To France 1906. *Breakfast.* 1914. Pasted paper, crayon, and oil on canvas, $31\frac{7}{8}$ x $23\frac{1}{2}$ inches. Acquired through the Lillie P. Bliss Bequest. [248.48]

Whereas Picasso had incorporated painted letters as an important element into the composition of his *"Ma Jolie"* (page 48), in the *Breakfast* Gris applied an actual snippet of newspaper to his canvas, together with other pieces of textured paper. A few years before, Picasso and Braque, the cofounders of Cubism, had begun to introduce extraneous materials into their works in a technique known as "collage" (from the French *coller,* to paste). Soon both artists were affixing fragments of cloth, paper, and other substances to the surfaces of their pictures. Besides en-

riching the textures, this was a blow at traditional notions of the medium of painting. It was also a way of asserting the primacy of the constructed work of art as an object in its own right, not an illusionistic representation of something already existing in the natural world.

Gris, the third leading master of Cubism, quickly adopted this device and made it his own. In the *Breakfast,* he indulged in eye-fooling tricks, challenging us to distinguish the actual bits of pasted paper from those simulated with crayon and paint. Slyly, he selected from the newspaper a piece including his own name.

The objects in the *Breakfast* are more easily recognizable than those in the *"Ma Jolie."* They are drawn with definite outlines and modeled in light and shade, though partially fragmented and shown from several incompatible angles of vision. The way in which the top of the table is tilted toward us so that we can look down on the objects from above is derived from Cézanne's still lifes (such as the one on page 30).

Gris constructed his picture by dissecting various objects and then organizing them into a synthetic image of his subject. Instead of painting with monochromatic grays and browns within a gridwork of horizontal and vertical lines, he cut out different shapes and arranged them, with mathematical precision and poetic sensibility, against his painted blue background, to create what he called "flat, colored architecture."

GEORGES BRAQUE. French, 1882–1963. *The Table.* 1928. Oil on canvas, 70¾ x 28¾ inches. Acquired through the Lillie P. Bliss Bequest. [520.41]

In *The Table,* Braque employed the Cubist devices of spatial ambiguity and fragmentation of forms to produce a richly decorative still life. The table is set back in space on a tiled floor, against the paneled dado of the wall, and its grooved pedestal and curved legs are rendered illusionistically. In the center and upper part of the picture, however, the table top is sharply tipped upward to display the gadrooned tray, guitar, newspaper, and compotier with fruit. Above, two oblong panels like an open screen are set flat against the wall; the blue and black of these panels are continued below the table, but in the form of transparent shadows, on which the paneling is shown by white outlines like those of a photograph negative.

The composition is divided by a distinct vertical axis that emphasizes the high, narrow proportions of the canvas. The objects on the table are broken up into a complex design, in which many small areas of dark and light are used to create a rhythmic, ornamental effect rather than a sense of solidity. White and black set off the limited but subtle color scheme—browns, tans, grays, light yellow, and deep blue. The texture is enriched by sand mixed with the pigment to produce a mat, grainy surface.

51

ROGER DE LA FRESNAYE. French, 1885–1925. *The Conquest of the Air.* 1913. Oil on canvas, 7 feet 8⅞ inches x 6 feet 5 inches. Mrs. Simon Guggenheim Fund. [222.47]

In this large painting, La Fresnaye used Cubism's geometrized form and dissected space to create a monumental composition on an heroic theme. In the treatment of the sky, with its overlapping planes of clear color and its globular clouds, there are also some reminiscences of Delaunay (compare the *Sun and Moon,* page 33).

Aviation was still in its pioneering stage when this picture was painted. In 1908, Wilbur Wright had broken records with a 56-mile, 140-minute flight from La Fresnaye's native town of Le Mans, and in the following year Blériot made the first air crossing of the Channel. La Fresnaye's interest in aviation was more than casual, for his brother Henri was director of the Nieuport aircraft manufacturing plant near Meulan, the village represented in the landscape at the lower left of the picture.

The two men seated at the table (possibly the artist himself and his brother) are engaged in conversation, presumably on the topic referred to in the title. That this is a conceptual rather than a representational treatment of the theme is evident by the disproportionately large size of the two figures and their indeterminate location with respect to the landscape. Furthermore, the tiny balloon floating aloft, its rounded shape repeating that of the clouds, is only a symbol of aeronautical triumphs and not a depiction of the most up-to-date technological advances. The sailboat at the right, besides connoting a favorite sport of the brothers, also suggests a parallel between man's intellectual ability to tame the forces of the wind so that he can navigate upon the waters, and his new mastery of air currents and the laws of aerodynamics that enable him to fly. The huge tricolor asserts La Fresnaye's nationalistic pride and confidence in the role that France is destined to play in the future of aviation. Between 1911 and 1914, he painted several pictures on patriotic themes, in which the French flag figures prominently, but none matches the spaciousness, balanced composition, and brilliant color of *The Conquest of the Air.*

MARC CHAGALL. French, born Russia 1887. To France 1923. In U.S.A. 1941–1948. *I and the Village.* 1911. Oil on canvas, 6 feet 3⅝ inches x 59⅝ inches. Mrs. Simon Guggenheim Fund. [146.45]

Chagall came to Paris from Russia in 1910 and remained for several years. Like La Fresnaye, he was quick to make use of Delaunay's brilliant color and Cubism's superimposition of fragmented objects freely arranged within a flattened space, adapting these devices as means with which to give full rein to his exuberant fantasy.

This is the first of Chagall's paintings called *I and the Village,* of which he made numerous replicas; the title was supplied by the poet Blaise Cendrars. It is a memory picture of his native Vitebsk, composed of dreamlike images that totally disregard naturalistic color, relative size, and even the laws of gravity. The large head of a farm animal in white, black, gray, blue, and pink encloses a vignette of a cow being milked and confronts the profile of Chagall himself as a capped peasant, painted green with white highlights. The segmented circle uniting the two heads is intersected below by a triangle enframing a nosegay upheld in the peasant's huge fingers. At the top of the canvas, against a cloud-filled, many-hued sky, appears a panorama of the village's church, houses, and inhabitants—some upside down!

In a discussion of this picture, the critic Robert Rosenblum has pointed out: "The physical restrictions of the seen world give way to the psychological release of an imagined world, but this new-found liberty is balanced by the new-found discipline of Cubism. . . . Chagall's seemingly random associations . . . are tightly fused in a centrifugal fabric of interlocking Cubist planes . . . joining these fragments in a coherent whole."

UMBERTO BOCCIONI. Italian, 1882–1916. *Dynamism of a Soccer Player.* 1913. Oil on canvas, 6 feet 4⅛ inches x 6 feet 7⅛ inches. The Sidney and Harriet Janis Collection. [580.67]

Bursting upon the vision like an exploding pinwheel, Boccioni's *Dynamism of a Soccer Player* conveys an immediate impression of furious energy, even before one deciphers the figure of the running athlete that is its embodiment. As described by Marianne W. Martin: "In this painting there is an inward-turning spiral—suggestive of the figure's mainspring of energy—which begins with the pointed, wing-like hand on the left, passes the head, the left thigh, and ends in the region of the groin (the geometric centre), to which the downward passage of the left light calls attention. This motion is immediately countered by the three major, slightly angular arcs which emerge from this core. They describe the progressive extension of the smoothly interlocking members of the athlete's body into the environment. . . . The bright, translucent colours and the calculated use of light help both to retard and to intensify the suggestion of disintegration of form through motion by heightening or destroying the effects of solidity. The luminous blue wedges of 'sky' cut right through the player, making his steely limbs apparently weightless; they seem to lift him into the air where he hurtles and spins, his barely visible head protected by powerful shoulder blades."

Boccioni was one of five painters (two others being Severini, page 43, and Balla, page 96) who, inspired by the ideas of the poet Tommaso Marinetti, issued the Futurist Painting: Technical Manifesto in 1910. Besides asserting their rebellion against academic art, they proclaimed allegiance to all that was most forceful in modern life. They outlined the principles that would guide their painting: "The gesture which we would reproduce on canvas shall no longer be a fixed *moment* in universal dynamism. It shall simply be the dynamic sensation itself. Indeed, all things move, all things run, all things are rapidly changing. . . . On account of the persistency of an image upon the retina, moving objects constantly multiply themselves; their form changes like rapid vibrations, in their mad career. . . . To paint a human figure you must not paint it; you must render the whole of its surrounding atmosphere." In order to heighten the radiance of their colors and make even the shadows luminous, the Futurists adopted Seurat's technique of applying pigment in dots (see page 17), or used tiny strokes.

Painted in 1913, the *Dynamism of a Soccer Player* is in itself a visual manifesto of the goals enunciated three years before. In its shallow space and shifting, transparent planes, it also reveals the influence of Analytical Cubism (see page 48), with which Boccioni had become familiar on a visit to Paris in 1911. It exemplifies, too, another principle, which he set forth in the following year: that of making the spectator a participant in the action by painting "lines of force" to encircle and involve him, "so that he will in a manner be forced to struggle himself with the persons in the picture."

The year before he painted the *Dynamism of a Soccer Player,* Boccioni issued the Technical Manifesto of Futurist Sculpture, applying Futurist theories to that medium. The object was no longer to be conceived as a representation, but as a construction of planes and volumes—the nucleus of dynamic forces prolonging themselves into the surrounding space. The *Unique Forms of Continuity in Space* of 1912–1913 in The Museum of Modern Art is the climactic realization of these principles. In this modern counterpart of the winged *Victory of Samothrace,* Boccioni anticipated the running athlete of the *Dynamism of a Soccer Player* with a three-dimensional, striding figure, altering naturalistic forms to express the speed with which the powerful body thrusts its way through the atmosphere.

MARCEL DUCHAMP. American, born France. 1887–1968. Active in New York 1915–1918, 1920–1923, 1942–1968. *The Passage from Virgin to Bride.* 1912. Oil on canvas, 23⅜ x 21¼ inches. Purchase. [174.45]

While still in his twenties, Duchamp determined to "get away from the physical aspect of painting" in order to create ideas rather than mere "visual products." Since he "wanted to put painting once again at the service of the mind," he gave special importance to the titles of his works. The title of this picture refers to the rite of passage, the transition undergone by a young woman in passing from the virginal to the married state. Many years later, Duchamp observed that, in a sense, the painting also marked his "own passage from something into something else"—notably, from Cubism and his former attachment to traditional means of painting to a more dematerialized, intellectual concept, which he thought of as "reduction" rather than "abstraction."

In his famous *Nude Descending a Staircase,* now in the Philadelphia Museum of Art, Duchamp had attempted to give "a static representation of movement" in a manner he considered "closer to the Cubists' interest in decomposing forms than to the Futurists' interest in suggesting movement." Here, since his theme was not physical motion but the metamorphosis of a woman from one state of being to another, he represented her in two different aspects. She is shown as an ambiguous fusion of the organic and the mechanical. At the left, as the Virgin, she resembles the figure in the *Nude Descending a Staircase,* with inclined head, long spinal column, and bent knee. To the right, she becomes the Bride, assuming a form that Duchamp would repeat, with variations, in other works of 1912 and the next few years, culminating in his "Large Glass," *The Bride Stripped Bare by Her Bachelors, Even.* Though the colors here still relate to the monochromy of such Cubist works as Picasso's *"Ma Jolie"* (page 48), they are tinged with warmer, pinkish tones, appropriate to the organic nature of the humanoid machine (compare Picabia's *I See Again in Memory My Dear Udnie,* page 44).

Like Duchamp's related paintings on the theme of the Bride, this picture is packed with metaphors and arcane allusions. Some he himself has elucidated, while others have given rise to as much "explication" as the writings of James Joyce. Duchamp's disavowal of the "physical side of painting" notwithstanding, the viewer who lacks any key with which to decode *The Passage from Virgin to Bride* can nevertheless be fascinated by the subtleties of its rich, though subdued, coloring, the sensuousness of its shading and its glossy surface, and the intricate play of its convex and concave forms.

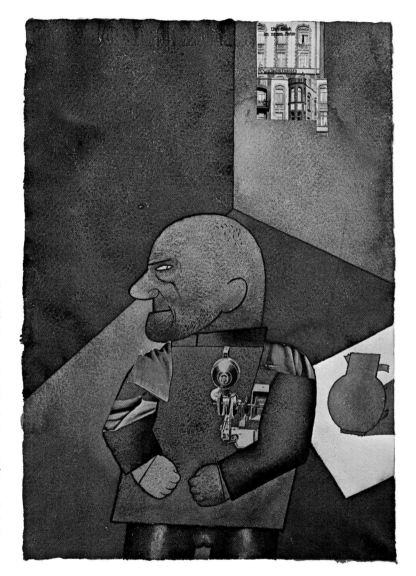

GEORGE GROSZ, American. 1893–1959. Born and died in Germany. In U.S.A. 1932–1959. *The Engineer Heartfield.* 1920. Watercolor and collage of pasted postcard and halftone, $16\frac{1}{2}$ x 12 inches. Gift of A. Conger Goodyear. [176.52]

In contrast to Duchamp and Picabia (page 44), who were interested in exploring the machine's erotic implications, a group of artists in Germany after the First World War glorified the machine as a means for constructing a new utopian society. They had become familiar with the antiart principles of the international Dada movement, founded in Zurich in 1916, and quickly adapted them for their own revolutionary aims. Their particular target of attack was the bourgeoisie and the military leadership, which they held responsible for Germany's disastrous defeat. On the positive side, they wished to emulate Soviet Russia's emphasis on technology and were especially influenced by the ideas of the influential Constructivist, Vladimir Tatlin.

Grosz's portrait represents one of the leading figures among the German Dadaists, John Heartfield. He had anglicized his name, Hans Herzfelde, as an antinationalist gesture, just as Grosz spelled his first name "George" in the English manner. Both men took part in a demonstration at the First International Dada Fair in Berlin in June, 1920, carrying a sign that proclaimed "Art is dead—long live Tatlin's new machine art." This picture, probably a gift from Grosz to his friend, makes ironic reference to one of the several times that Heartfield was imprisoned for political activities. His villainous appearance conforms to his habit of shaving only one cheek, on the pretext of suffering from a skin disease, and of further dishonoring the army uniform by continuing, after his demobilization, to wear a particularly shabby, dirty one.

Grosz has portrayed Heartfield in a cell, on the back wall of which is a sign wishing him "lots of luck in his new home." Pinned to his breast like a medal is a "machine-heart," symbol of his attachment to the concept of bringing about a new, rational, technological society.

The Engineer Heartfield uses pasted-on elements in a technique called "photomontage," which was elaborated by the Berlin Dadaists. It was a type of collage utilizing images cut from many sources, such as newspapers, magazines, or postcards, and derived from a device of German army photographers, who inserted portrait heads in oleographic mounts of idealized settings. The use of ready-made materials taken from mass media was in itself a kind of "antiart" in keeping with Dada tenets.

KURT SCHWITTERS. British subject, born Germany. 1887–1948. To England 1940. *Picture with Light Center.* 1919. Collage of paper with oil on cardboard, 33¼ x 25⅞ inches. Purchase. [18.50]

Though closely associated for a time with some of the German Dadaists (see page 57), Schwitters was opposed both to their political orientation and their antiart position. In spite of using in his collages bits of paper and other scraps picked up on the street or gathered from trashcans or wastebaskets, Schwitters always insisted that his aims were aesthetic, and that the form of his compositions was more essential than the materials of which they were made. "I could not, in fact, see the reason why old tickets, driftwood, cloakroom tabs, wires and parts of wheels, buttons and old rubbish found in attics and refuse dumps should not be as suitable a material for painting as the paints made in factories," he declared. "I called my new works utilizing such materials MERZ. This is the second syllable of *Kommerz.* It originated in . . . a work in which the word *Merz,* cut out from an advertisement of the Kommerz und Privatbank and pasted on, could be read among the abstract elements. . . . Merz stands for freedom from all fetters. . . . Freedom is not lack of restraint, but the product of strict artistic discipline."

The use of scraps of material had, of course, been anticipated in Cubist collage (see page 50), but Schwitters, as William Rubin has pointed out, "broadened the range of its vocabulary and conjured from it a unique and nostalgic poetry." The *Picture with Light Center* combines a central radiating pattern like that found in some Futurist works, such as Boccioni's *Dynamism of a Soccer Player* (page 55), with vertical and horizontal accents related to the underlying rectilinear grid of such Cubist compositions as Picasso's *"Ma Jolie"* (page 48). Here, some sections have been painted in oil, but in his later works, which are usually smaller in size, Schwitters tended to use pasted-on elements exclusively.

ARTHUR G. DOVE. American, 1880–1946. *Grandmother.* 1925. Collage of shingles, needlepoint, page from the Concordance, pressed flowers, and ferns, 20 x 21¼ inches. Gift of Philip L. Goodwin (by exchange). [636.39]

The stamps, bits of tickets, and other scraps in Schwitters' collages were selected and arranged solely for their color, form, and texture and not because they had any intrinsic significance. Each of the elements in Dove's *Grandmother,* however, was chosen for its specific connotations. Alfred H. Barr, Jr. has described it: "The artist in making his composition has taken a page from an old Bible concordance, some pressed ferns and flowers, a piece of faded needlepoint embroidery and a row of weathered shingles turned silvery grey with age; these he has com-bined into a *visual poem,* each element, each metaphor of which suggests some aspect of the idea of grand-mother: her age, her fragility, her silvery hair, her patience, her piety."

The fragments are arranged in a more rigidly recti-linear pattern than those in Schwitters' *Picture with Light Center;* the textures, on the other hand, are considerably more varied. It has been pointed out that Dove's collages probably owe less to the sophisticated use of this medium in Europe than to the American nineteenth-century folk-art tradition of creating assemblages with various materials having associations with their subject. The folk artists, however, usually aimed at representation and vis-ual likeness, whereas Dove's collages are abstract and place greater emphasis on compositional unity.

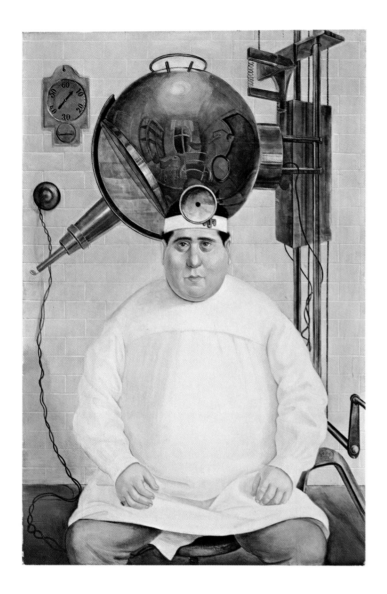

OTTO DIX. German, 1891–1969. *Dr. Mayer-Hermann.* 1926. Oil and tempera on wood, 58¾ x 39 inches. Gift of Philip Johnson. [3.32]

Compared to Dove's symbolic portrayal of his grandmother (page 59), Dix's portrait of Dr. Wilhelm Mayer-Hermann seems highly realistic, though in actuality its composition and manner of painting are artfully stylized. The precise draughtsmanship and even finish, giving equal emphasis to all details, have precedents in the work of such German old masters as Cranach and Holbein.

The subject, a prominent Berlin throat specialist, is presented in strict frontality, surrounded by accessories that echo his conspicuous rotundity. His round face, with half-moons under the eyes, bulbous nose, pursed mouth with full underlip, and double chin, rises directly, without any indication of his neck, above the arched shoulders that slope into the curved arms enframing his corpulent torso. Though the characterization verges on satire, we sense in it no malice.

The roundness of the instrument strapped onto the doctor's forehead is repeated in enlarged scale by the spherical X-ray apparatus behind his head. The polished surface of this globe reflects a distorted image of the clinic. The circular motif is picked up by the outlet on the wall at the left, the clock face above it, and the medallion on the base of the machine at the lower right, which encloses the artist's monogram and the date.

Dix was one of a number of German painters who, after the end of the First World War and the social upheaval that followed it, reacted from expressionism, abstraction, Dada protest, and fantasy to concentrate upon the realistic depiction of the material world. Underlying their short-lived movement, called the New Objectivity, was an attitude of resigned cynicism—an acceptance of things as they are, rather than as they ought to be.

Fernando Botero. Colombian, born 1932. In U.S.A. since 1961. *Mona Lisa, Age Twelve.* 1959. Oil and tempera on canvas, 6 feet 11⅛ inches x 6 feet 5 inches. Inter-American Fund. [279.61]

In Botero's portrait, the chubbiness of the sitter is more humorously exaggerated than in Dix's *Dr. Mayer-Hermann.* The effect of caricature is heightened by the manner in which the inflated image of the head, set above disproportionately small arms and hands, fills almost the entire surface of the large canvas.

This is one of a series of six paintings in which Botero represented Mona Lisa at different ages. He has said: "Leonardo's *Mona Lisa* is so popular that perhaps it is no longer art. It is like a movie star or a football player. Hence an obvious satirical element in my painting. . . . While doing this painting, I discovered that what is important is not the *smile,* but the eyes."

Born in Colombia, Botero studied in Europe, where he was influenced by the old masters' technique of modeling forms in light and shade in a manner that has been abandoned in much of recent art, and by their use of oil and tempera combined. Dix also used tempera and oil together (though on a wood support rather than on canvas), but the cold tonality and enamellike finish of his painting is in direct contrast to the way in which Botero lays on fresh, lively colors with large brushstrokes that evidence his sensuous delight in his medium.

61

OSKAR KOKOSCHKA. British subject, born Austria 1886 of Austrian-Czech parents. Worked in Germany and Czechoslovakia. To England 1938. Lives in Switzerland. *Hans Tietze and Erica Tietze-Conrat.* 1909. Oil on canvas, 30⅛ x 53⅝ inches. Abby Aldrich Rockefeller Fund. [651.39]

The double portrait, a traditional subject in art, has here been given a twentieth-century interpretation that emphasizes the psychological relationship between the sitters rather than merely transcribing their physical characteristics. The painting was commissioned by the art historians Hans Tietze and Erica Tietze-Conrat for the overmantel of their house in Vienna when they, and Kokoschka, were young.

The artist has stated that he sought "to render the vision of being alive, owing to the effect of an inner light," in a creative approach diametrically opposed to "theories of art that assert that the human being should be seen as a kind of *nature morte.*" Light does indeed seem to emanate from these figures. The striated lines that surround them are like rays, and the thinly painted, high-keyed color of the background, with its mysterious incised graffiti, envelops the pair in its atmosphere.

The couple do not look directly at each other. Their intimate communion is more subtly expressed by the sensitively drawn, nervous hands. As in Michelangelo's *Creation of Adam* in the ceiling of the Sistine Chapel, an electric tension is generated between the fingers that approach closely without quite touching.

BALTHUS (Baltusz Klossowski de Rola). French, born 1908. *Joan Miró and His Daughter Dolores.* 1937–1938. Oil on canvas, 51¼ x 35 inches. Abby Aldrich Rockefeller Fund. [398.38]

This double portrait, which is at the opposite pole from Kokoschka's, would probably fall into the category of those he scornfully characterized as "still life." Balthus stubbornly adhered to the realist tradition and, taking the nineteenth-century artist Courbet as his model, painstakingly sought to render an exact physical likeness of his sitters. For this painting, Miró and his daughter posed nearly every day for three months. In order to make them stay still, Balthus rigged up wooden blocks

to hold their feet in place—undoubtedly an ordeal for a lively little girl, and probably for her father, too, judging by his rather set expression.

The tender relationship between father and daughter, as well as the resemblance between them, nevertheless comes through. Again, as in the case of Kokoschka's married couple, it is conveyed principally by the position of the hands—Miró's showing the gentlest restraint, Dolores' a confiding affection. The horizontal line marking the juncture of floor and wall divides the composition precisely midway. The sober, unornamented background, without a single detail to detract attention from the figures, serves as foil to the vertical stripes and red piping of the child's dress.

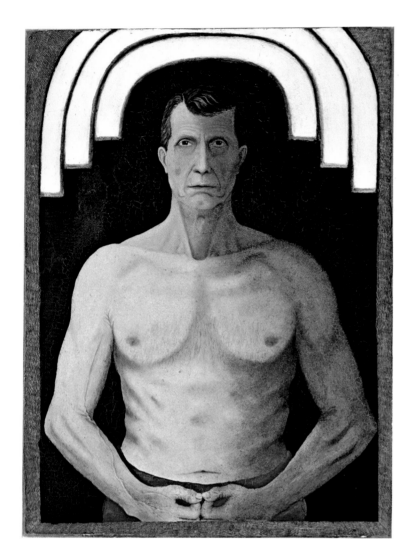

JOHN KANE. American, born Scotland. 1860–1934. To U.S.A. 1880. *Self-Portrait.* 1929. Oil on canvas over composition board, 36⅛ x 27⅛ inches. Abby Aldrich Rockefeller Fund. [6.39]

The subject of this self-portrait stares out at us with unflinching directness; we recognize that the artist's aim was to paint his own image as realistically as possible. At the same time, he has given his composition a strong sense of design through the formal, symmetrical pose; the patterning of the sinews, veins, muscles, and bony framework of the gaunt torso; the triple arch above; and the painted frame with its simulated wood graining. Taken together, these devices and the manner in which the figure is offset against its dark background call to mind North European portraits of the fifteenth and early sixteenth centuries.

Kane came to this country from Scotland at the age of twenty and worked as miner, laborer, carpenter, steelworker, and construction foreman. As he said in his autobiography, he did "almost every kind of work a laboring man can do. . . . The amount of work, the hardness of it, the hours and all like that, didn't worry me a bit. . . . I liked to work and I did not care how hard it was. I think I rather enjoyed using my strong muscles." He also used them to gain considerable renown as a fist fighter.

These strenuous activities had to be abandoned when Kane lost a leg in a railroad accident. After working as a railroad watchman, he got a job painting freight cars. From this experience, he "learned the use of lead paint, the mixing of colors, the necessity of keeping colors clean and a deal else of information"—a training that he declared was far better than any he might have received in an art school. As a self-taught artist, he devoted every possible moment of his spare time to drawing and painting, bringing to his art the same painstaking care that he had exercised as a laborer; "I think a painting has a right to be as exact as a joist or a mold or any other part of building construction," he said.

Apart from recollections of his Scottish homeland, Kane's favorite subjects were scenes of Pittsburgh; he saw beauty not only in its surrounding countryside but also in its industrial landscape. This, one of his rare portraits, took him two years to complete; it dates from the time when his art first began to win recognition, following acceptance of one of his paintings for the Carnegie International Exhibition in 1927.

Kane was a man of profound piety and dignity. That, at sixty-nine, he still prided himself on his probity, self-reliance, and manly strength is quite evident from the straightforwardness of his gaze, and his pose, designed to emphasize the tension of his flexed muscles. He brings to mind another honest stalwart, Longfellow's village blacksmith:

The smith, a mighty man is he,
With large and sinewy hands;
And the muscles of his brawny arms
Are strong as iron bands. . . .
His brow is wet with honest sweat,
He earns whate'er he can,
And looks the whole world in the face,
For he owes not any man.

KAREL APPEL. Dutch, born 1921. In Paris since 1950. *Étienne-Martin.* 1956. Oil on canvas, 6 feet 4⅞ inches x 51¼ inches. Purchase. [183.66]

The large bearded head with fiercely intense gaze, and the manner in which it is brought forward to the surface of the canvas and closely fitted within the oblong format, give Appel's portrait of the sculptor Henri Étienne-Martin the aspect of an icon. With expressionist exuberance, Appel has built up the image by combining a tangle of calligraphic lines with heavy globs of paint laid on with the palette knife. "My paint tube is like a rocket which describes its own space," he said. "I try to make the impossible possible. What is happening I cannot foresee; it is a surprise. Painting, like passion, is an emotion full of truth and rings a living sound, like the roar coming from the lion's breast."

In 1948, Appel and two other young Dutch painters in Amsterdam founded the Experimental Group, which soon made contact with similarly inclined artists from Denmark and Belgium. Together, they published a magazine, to which they gave the same name as their group, COBRA (an acronym for Copenhagen, Brussels, Amsterdam). Though they shared with the Surrealists an admiration for primitive, folk, schizophrenic, and child art, they were more optimistic in their outlook and more committed to the "act of creation" as the fundamental experience in art. Thus, Appel declared: "I never try to make a painting, but a chunk of life. It is a scream; it is a night; it is like a child; it is a tiger behind bars."

After moving to Paris in 1950, Appel began to participate in exhibitions with other artists who were also engaged in evolving a type of representational art that was strongly emotive, nonrational, and counter to traditional aesthetic values. They were especially concerned with the sensuous properties of the paint medium itself—the color and substance of pigment and its textural enlivenment of the picture's surface.

A comparison with photographs of Étienne-Martin shows that Appel retained the sitter's physical likeness to a surprising degree. The emphasis on the creative process that brought the painting into being nevertheless asserts the identity of the artist perhaps even more strongly than that of his subject. The over-life-size dimensions of this portrait reinforce the aggressiveness of its confrontation with the viewer.

FERNAND LÉGER. French, 1881–1955. In U.S.A. 1940–1945. *Exit the Ballets Russes.* 1914. Oil on canvas, 53¾ x 39½ inches. Gift of Mr. and Mrs. Peter A. Rübel. [11.58]

By 1913, Léger had absorbed the lessons of Cézanne's treatment of form and color and Cubism's underlying geometrical structure, and had developed an abstract style of his own that emphasized contrasts of colors, lines, volumes, and planes. He restricted his range of colors to create greater contrasts between the forms. In the *Exit the Ballets Russes,* for example, he used only red, blue, green, yellow, and brown for the figures and stairway, giving his shapes firm black outlines and strong white highlights to emphasize their solidity.

Léger treated the subject of the staircase in several paintings at about this date, possibly in recollection of Duchamp's famous *Nude Descending a Staircase* of 1911, but primarily because the theme allowed him to impart a rhythmic sense of movement in space to his articulated, geometrical forms. In this painting, human beings are transformed into robots made up of cylinders and cones, with ovoid heads. Subsequently, Léger's wartime experience in the army increased his admiration for the beauty of machines, and he developed a style in which both figures and objects are rendered as depersonalized, tubular forms, as in the *Three Women* (page 71). Here, despite the machinelike personages, the everyday subject is more realistic and less conceptual than Duchamp's *Passage from Virgin to Bride* (page 56) or Picabia's *I See Again in Memory My Dear Udnie* (page 44).

The *Exit the Ballets Russes* was formerly owned by the famous dancer and choreographer Léonid Massine, who became a member of Diaghilev's troupe in the same year that Léger painted the picture.

OSKAR SCHLEMMER. German, 1888–1943. *Bauhaus Stairway.* 1932. Oil on canvas, 63⅞ inches x 45 inches. Gift of Philip Johnson. [597.42]

Schlemmer's subject, figures on a stairway, is the same as that of Léger's *Exit the Ballets Russes,* which it also resembles in its general proportions and color range. Though the idealized forms are drastically simplified, the personages are not transformed, as are Léger's, into automata.

The light-filled interior with its large windows and glass stair parapet is an actual depiction of the architecture of the Bauhaus at Dessau, the pioneering school of art and technology founded by Walter Gropius, which in the late 'twenties and early 'thirties led the world in the field of modern design. Schlemmer painted the picture from memory in Breslau on the basis of earlier studies, three years after leaving the Bauhaus, where he had been instructor in theater and ballet. The dancer *en pointe* in the background recalls the latter activity.

The two side figures and the lower one seen from the rear, all cut by the frame, give the viewer the impression of being a participant in the upward movement. By making the architecture that he represented seem a continuation of the real space we occupy, Schlemmer made his paintings a close-knit part of their surroundings.

The *Bauhaus Stairway* was the principal painting in an exhibition of Schlemmer's work in his native town of Stuttgart in 1933. Ten days after the show opened, it was closed by the Nazis on the charge of "art bolshevism," and Schlemmer was dismissed from his professorship at the Breslau Academy. The Bauhaus at Dessau had already been closed by the authorities the preceding year.

HENRI MATISSE. French, 1869–1954. *Piano Lesson.* 1916. Oil on canvas, 8 feet ½ inch x 6 feet 11¾ inches. Mrs. Simon Guggenheim Fund. [125.46]

The subject of the *Piano Lesson*—an inhabited interior, with a view through an open casement to a garden beyond—is basically the same as that of Bonnard's *Breakfast Room* (page 27). But whereas Bonnard's painting represents an extension of the Impressionist tradition, the rigorous simplifications and geometrizing of forms in this picture are evidences of Matisse's assimilation of certain Cubist principles.

This very large picture shows Matisse's son Pierre practicing on the Pleyel in the living room of the family villa at Issy-les-Moulineaux, a suburb of Paris. His back is turned to the green foliage of the garden glimpsed through the open window, and he seems a reluctant captive barricaded by the piano in front of him and guarded by the austere figure seated behind him, who looks down as if in surveillance. She is not a real woman, however, but an elongated version of one of Matisse's paintings of 1914, the *Woman on a High Stool.* This clothed and rigid personage in dull blue, gray, black, and white wittily complements the relaxed brown nude in the lower left corner—Matisse's bronze *Decorative Figure* of 1908.

As Alfred H. Barr, Jr. has pointed out: "The painting is full of other subtle analogies and entertaining polarities. Besides the two intricately contrasted female figures, the big triangle of green, as it echoes and expands the small foreground triangle of the metronome, may be noted; and also the play between the black arabesques of music rack and window grill. The sharp converging points of green, black, pink and gray provide a valuable moment of excitement in an otherwise disciplined calm, just as the vigorously pyramidal metronome disturbs the general flatness of the rest of the picture."

68

PABLO PICASSO. Spanish, 1881–1973. To France 1904. *Three Musicians.* 1921. Oil on canvas, 6 feet 7 inches x 7 feet 3¾ inches. Mrs. Simon Guggenheim Fund. [55.49]

Picasso began to provide decor for Diaghilev's Ballets Russes in 1917; and in 1920, the year before this picture was painted, he designed the costumes for *Pulcinella,* a ballet based on the old commedia dell'arte with a score by Stravinsky adapted from music by Pergolesi.

Within a stagelike space, the *Three Musicians* sets two commedia dell'arte characters, Pierrot and Harlequin, together with a third, mysteriously veiled figure at the right, who wears a domino or a monk's garb. Beneath the table before them at the left sprawls a dog, its body as fragmented as are those of the three musicians.

In spite of the indications of a floor and walls, the picture is uncompromisingly two-dimensional. The figures are made up of flat, zigzag shapes that recall those in earlier Cubist pictures using cut-and-pasted papers, such as Gris' *Breakfast* (page 50). Here, however, the composition is of monumental scale, and, notwithstanding the implicit gaiety of its subject, the total effect is one of hieratic solemnity. This is owing, in large part, to the sobriety of the color scheme, in which black, brown, and white predominate. The brighter colors—blue, reddish-orange, and yellow—are concentrated in the center of the picture. The tiny, clawlike hands emphasize both the large size of the figures and the complete subordination of their anatomy to geometrized forms.

FERNAND LÉGER. French, 1881–1955. In U.S.A. 1940–1945. *Three Women.* 1921. Oil on canvas, 6 feet ¼ inch x 8 feet 3 inches. Mrs. Simon Guggenheim Fund. [189.42]

Painted in the same year as Picasso's *Three Musicians,* Léger's *Three Women* is of almost the same dimensions and presents a similar subject—three personages within an interior, seen in strict frontality. (The cat may even be regarded as a counterpart of Picasso's dog!) But whereas Picasso's geometrized figures are wholly flat and weightless, and are drawn with angular contours, Léger's are solid, heavy, and curvilinear. Though the women are more recognizably human than the robots in his earlier *Exit the Ballets Russes* (page 66), they reflect an even greater admiration for machinelike forms. The severely simplified, rounded heads and bodies are as highly pol-

ished as if made of metal. With their impassive faces and static poses, and the white, black, gray, and brown tones in which they are painted, the three women seem almost more inanimate than the brightly patterned decor and accessory objects that surround them.

Léger said this picture expressed the "classical" rather than "romantic" side of his art; choice of a conventional theme let him focus on pictorial means instead of subject. Simplification of forms and emphasis on volumes does, in fact, go back beyond Cubist abstraction to one of the major traditions within French art. This classic style is notably exemplified in the work of the seventeenth-century artist Poussin, who tended to repress emotionalism and sensuousness in his paintings for the sake of a strictly organized compositional structure and a disciplined harmony between human figures and their setting.

JOAN MIRÓ. Spanish, born 1893. In Paris 1919–1940. *Dutch Interior, I.* 1928. Oil on canvas, 36⅛ x 28¾ inches. Mrs. Simon Guggenheim Fund. [163.45]

The traditional subject of an interior with figures is further explored in the paintings reproduced on this and the following pages. On a visit to Holland in 1928, Miró was attracted by genre paintings of this theme as rendered by the seventeenth-century Dutch "Little Masters" and brought back a number of postcards of their works. The *Dutch Interior, I* is the first of three compositions in which he freely adapted pictures of this type.

Sorgh's *Lute Player,* which formed the basis for the Museum's painting, shows a swain with brimmed hat seated with crossed legs, playing his lute to a lady who leans with one elbow resting upon a table laid with a cloth, fruit bowl, wine glass, and dish. In the foreground are a cat and a dog; at the left, a window opens out onto a view of Amsterdam. A painting hangs on the rear wall, with the narrow arches of interior windows above it.

All these details have been completely transformed in Miró's gay, brightly colored interior. In spite of the indications of space given by the wall, ceiling, and floor and the three-dimensionality of the window embrasure, the room, together with the figures and objects it contains, is essentially flat. Ribbonlike arabesques, wholly arbitrary patches of color, and patterning in areas of black and white take the place of modeling. In addition to his metamorphosis of the individual components in Sorgh's painting, Miró altered the everyday atmosphere of his prototype and turned it into fantasy by introducing a number of elements of his own invention, such as the footprint at the right, the bat flying above, and the bird swooping down from the ceiling.

GEORGES BRAQUE. French, 1882–1963. *Woman with a Mandolin.* 1937. Oil on canvas, 51¼ x 38¼ inches. Mrs. Simon Guggenheim Fund. [2.48]

Like Miró's *Dutch Interior,* Braque's painting shows a figure seated in a room playing a stringed instrument, with a picture hanging on the rear wall. Both works also freely interpolate three-dimensional elements into an essentially flat composition. The two paintings are entirely different, however, in their mood, style, and total effect. In contrast to the areas of flat color that provide a background for the figures and objects in Miró's painting, every part of the *Woman with a Mandolin* is filled with complex forms and designs. The woman is shown as a black silhouette, with the contours paralleled by white lines. A lighter shape appears behind her like an astral presence. The elongated form of the woman becomes assimilated into the total decor of the room, fusing with the

many other vertical accents throughout the composition, such as the chair back and legs, the music stand, and the bands of wallpaper ornamented with diverse patterns. The three-dimensionality suggested by the music stand, fluted lamp base with pleated shade, and frame of the still life at the left is denied in the right half of the picture, in which the elements are flatter and harder to decipher.

According to some interpretations, the dark figure of the woman accompanied by the lighter form behind it has a psychological significance analogous to the two images of the girl and her reflection in Picasso's *Girl before a Mirror* (page 76). It may, however, be simply a variant of the double view often used by the Cubists to show different aspects of a figure simultaneously.

Henri Matisse. French, 1869–1954. *The Red Studio.* 1911. Oil on canvas, 71¼ inches x 7 feet 2¼ inches. Mrs. Simon Guggenheim Fund. [8.49]

Matisse frequently introduced his own works into his paintings, as he did in the *Piano Lesson* (page 69). Here, in a boldly inventive, complex composition, the private world of his creations and possessions becomes the dominant subject. He has presented, in miniature scale and approximately their true colors, a selection of his paintings, sculptures, and ceramics—among them, to the right of the chest of drawers, the same bronze *Decorative Figure* shown in the *Piano Lesson.* Like the nudes in the *Dance* (page 42), the objects are arranged in a ring, its pivotal point being the grandfather clock in the background.

Against the monochromatic ground of Pompeian red that both unifies the painting and emphasizes its surface, the articles of furniture, schematically indicated by yellow outlines, seem weightless and impalpable compared to the more "real" works of art and a few other objects—notably the artist's implements and vase with trailing green vine on the table at the left. Though there are vestiges of conventional perspective, the uniform, all-pervasive red tends to negate depth in the same way that outlining reduces the weight and volume of the furniture.

In this painting, the absence of Matisse himself from the scene may carry an implication that the artist lives most significantly through what he creates. Such a notion may gain support from the fact that the paintings and sculptures shown constitute a brief réprise, through works still in Matisse's possession, of his activity from about 1898 (the year in which the small *Corsican Landscape* leaning against the stacked frames to the left was probably painted) to 1911, the approximate date of the *Large Nude* (to the rear of the left wall), the *Purple Cyclamen* (the right-hand picture above the chest of drawers), the *Jeannette, IV* (the sculpture to the right of the *Decorative Figure*), and the year of *The Red Studio* itself. This roughly corresponds to the development of Matisse's painting beginning with his early radical departures from naturalistic color, through his Fauve period (see page 114), represented by the *Young Sailor, II* (above and to the right of the clock) and *Le Luxe, II* (the large painting in the upper right corner), to his current large, decorative compositions, such as the *Large Nude.* In sculpture, it ranges from two quite naturalistic, decorative bronzes of 1904 and 1908 to the bolder distortions of the *Jeannette, IV*—still in progress in 1911, and shown here in plaster.

PABLO PICASSO. Spanish, 1881–1973. To France 1904.
Painter and Model. 1928. Oil on canvas, 51⅛ x 64¼
inches. The Sidney and Harriet Janis Collection. [644.67]

Like Matisse in *The Red Studio,* Picasso in the *Painter
and Model* presents an interpretation of the relation between the artist and the works he creates which implies
that the latter may have the greater "reality." He also
comments upon the process whereby the natural world is
transformed into the world of art. As Harriet Janis has
pointed out: "The artist and his model are abstracted to
an advanced degree while the concept in the canvas on
the easel is in terms of realism. By this reversal in the
scheme of reality the extraordinary artist and model are
declared ordinary and the natural profile becomes the
astonishing product of the artist's invention."

The painter is seated at the right on a chair with curved
back, which is upholstered in a floral pattern and
adorned with a fringe. He holds a kidney-shaped palette
in his left hand and a brush or palette knife in his right.
His head is a two-toned oval split at the top, with the features arranged within an arrow shape; the two eyes are
superimposed on his nose, and the mouth is represented
as a vertical slit with small hairs on either side. A canvas

with a classical profile drawn upon it stands before him;
at his right is a window with a view of blue sky beyond.
On the opposite side of the easel is a table with a green
fruit on a red cloth. The model, shown in profile at the
left, is an ambiguous image, which has been variously
read as a full-length human figure or as a sculptured portrait bust on a stand, with the horizontal lines below the
neck representing the molding on its pedestal.

The composition, based on Cubist principles, is structured on a system of horizontals and verticals and is
dominated by repeated geometrical elements—rectangles, triangles, circles, parallel lines, and dots. The
overall flatness of the design is not compromised by the
implied depth of the moldings, the oblique placement of
the artist's canvas, or the sky beyond the window. The
color range is limited. As in Léger's *Three Women* (page
71), the human figures or their semblances (the artist, his
model, and the picture on the easel) are rendered in neutral black, white, and gray, while color—red, yellow,
blue, green, and brown—is reserved for the inanimate
objects. The paint is applied in a heavy impasto.

Among Picasso's many portrayals of the artist and his
model, *The Studio,* 1927–1928, in The Museum of Modern Art, is even more strictly geometrized than this.

75

PABLO PICASSO. Spanish, 1881–1973. To France 1904. *Girl before a Mirror.* 1932. Oil on canvas, 64 x 51¼ inches. Gift of Mrs. Simon Guggenheim. [2.38]

The fascination of this picture lies not only in its rich, stained-glass colors and decorative patterning of lozenges, circles, and stripes, but also in its psychological implications, which have given rise to a host of interpretations. Certainly, we have here no realistic, objective representation of a young girl engaged in the banal act of contemplating her own reflection. The face of the "real" girl at the left is young and rather expressionless; her features are those of Marie-Thérèse Walter, with whom Picasso had recently begun a liaison, and whom he frequently represented at this time. By contrast, the face reflected in the mirror seems older and, with its unfathomable stare, parted lips, and hawklike nose, at once more anxious, aggressive, and inscrutable. It suggests a mysterious aspect of the girl's personality—as she is, or as she may become.

The body of the girl has been described as "simultaneously clothed, nude, and X-rayed." The striping of her bathing costume is transformed, at the right, into a diagrammatic rib cage. Her intense awareness of her own sexuality is manifest in the emphasis on rounded breasts and the bulging belly enclosing a circular womb.

This picture is a modern re-creation of a traditional Vanity image, in which a woman gazing into a mirror sees herself reflected as a death's head. It has also been noted that the looking glass is of a type called in France *psyché* —the Greek word for soul. It thus relates to a popular belief that a mirror has magic properties and can reflect the inner self, rather than the outward likeness, of the person who peers into it.

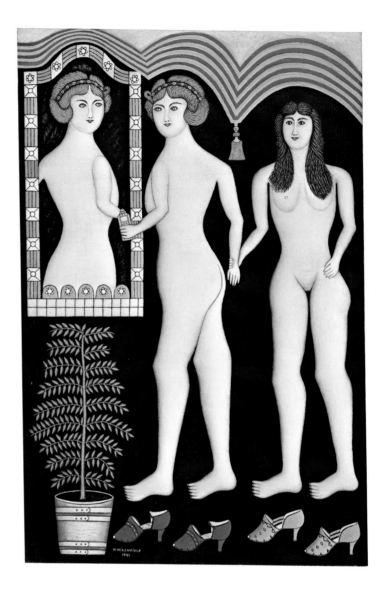

MORRIS HIRSHFIELD. American, born Russian Poland. 1872–1946. To U.S.A. 1890. *Inseparable Friends.* 1941. Oil on canvas, 60⅛ x 40⅛ inches. The Sidney and Harriet Janis Collection. [609.67]

No introspective musings trouble Hirshfield's young girl before a mirror, accompanied in unabashed nudity by her friend. Hirshfield came to the United States in his youth and, after working for several years in a woman's coat factory, became a manufacturer of boudoir slippers. He took up painting as a pastime at the age of sixty-five, when a severe illness forced him to retire from business. Like many self-taught artists, Hirshfield aimed at the literal rendition of reality; but, as he observed, at the outset "my mind knew well what I wanted to portray but my hands were unable to produce what my mind demanded." What he succeeded in achieving were compositions notable for their imaginative invention, rhythmic curves, and sense of texture.

Hirshfield was inspired to paint nudes by seeing Rousseau's *Dream* (page 80). In the *Inseparable Friends,* his second painting of nudes, he attempted a view of the front as well as the back, which he considered "even more beautiful." The reflection defies the laws of optics, for the mirror gives us another rear view of the girl who faces it.

Her smooth bust line swelling above a narrow waist and rounded hips is less suggestive of a human body than of a tailor's dummy, recalling one of Hirshfield's former occupations. The two pairs of slippers aligned at the bottom of the picture likewise remind us of his activity as a slipper manufacturer. Both girls have two left feet, which in spite of the difference in their poses are shown in profile.

The sense for decoration that Hirshfield shared with many primitive artists is apparent in the flowing lines of the pale bodies against the dark background, the red and blue slippers, the banded pot and symmetrical leaves of the plant, the ornamental framework of the mirror, the curves of the striped and tasseled canopy, and the carefully detailed strands of the girls' coiffures.

77

AMEDEO MODIGLIANI. Italian, 1884–1920. To France 1906. *Reclining Nude.* c. 1919. Oil on canvas, 28½ x 45⅞ inches. Mrs. Simon Guggenheim Fund. [13.50]

The reclining nude has been a favorite subject of painters ever since the Renaissance. The Italian-born Modigliani was a natural heir to this tradition and took the same delight in rendering the soft flesh, rounded swelling breasts, and sinuous curves of his model as did such old masters as Giorgione, Titian, and Veronese. The critic James Thrall Soby has observed that Modigliani's nudes "are an emphatic answer to his Futurist countrymen, who, infatuated with the machine, considered the subject outworn and urged its suppression for a period of ten years."

Modigliani, however, modernized his treatment of the theme by subtle simplifications and distortions—for example, the elongated torso and exaggerated outward thrust of the left hip. Modern, also, is the cutting off of the body by the framing edge of the canvas instead of showing it full length. The shadow that surrounds the figure emphasizes its flowing outline and enhances the contrast between the pale, evenly painted tones of the woman's body and the dark, rich colors and broken brushstrokes of the textured surface on which she lies.

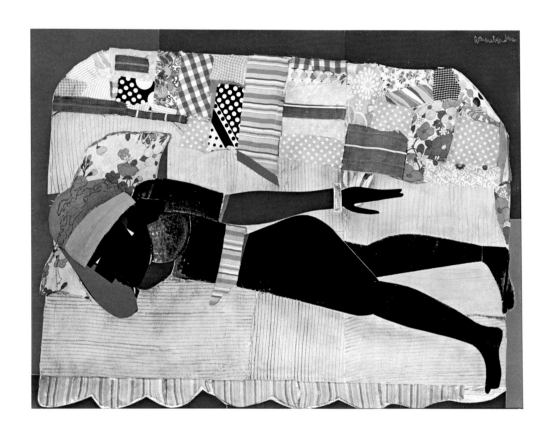

ROMARE BEARDEN. American, born 1914. *Patchwork Quilt.* 1970. Collage of cloth and paper with synthetic polymer paint on composition board, 35¾ x 47⅞ inches. Blanchette Rockefeller Fund. [573.70]

Bearden's treatment of the reclining nude is in complete contrast to Modigliani's. It certainly owes nothing to the classical tradition. A knowing student of many cultures, Bearden here seems to have found inspiration for his figure in ancient Egyptian sculpture. By turning the reproduction sideways, one can readily see how closely the proportions of the high-waisted body, the position of the legs, and the rendering of the left arm and hand resemble those in Egyptian tomb reliefs. The body seems carved out of granite instead of being molded of human flesh.

The sensuous appeal of this picture lies, rather, in the patchwork quilt for which it is named. The quilt is, of course, the product of a quite different culture—the folk art of rural America. Its bright, gay patterns provide a foil for the black figure, in a scheme that is the exact reversal of Modigliani's contrast of lights and darks.

Since the early 'sixties, Bearden has produced figurative subjects in collages of monumental scale. With obvious pleasure in color and design, he combines cloth, paper, and paint in sophisticated compositions, creating highly original images of forceful impact.

Henri Rousseau. French, 1844–1910. *The Dream.* 1910. Oil on canvas, 6 feet 8½ inches x 9 feet 9½ inches. Gift of Nelson A. Rockefeller. [252.54]

In contrast to the open spaces and few compositional elements in Rousseau's earlier painting *The Sleeping Gypsy* (page 13), the entire surface of *The Dream,* like some densely woven medieval tapestry, is filled with an allover pattern of branches, leaves, fruit, flowers, and animals. Once again we have a night scene illuminated by a full moon. At the left, in the midst of the jungle, a nude woman reclining on a sofa listens attentively to the music of a snake charmer. This incongruous apparition is explained by some verses that Rousseau attached to the painting when he sent it to the Salon des Indépendants for exhibition in 1910:

Yadwigha in a lovely dream,
Having most sweetly gone to sleep
Heard the snake-charmer blow his flute,
Breathing his meditation deep.

While on the streams and verdant trees
Gleam the reflections of the moon,
And savage serpents lend their ears
To the gay measures of the tune.

Yadwigha was the name of a Polish woman with whom Rousseau had been in love many years before. Although in his verses and in a letter he wrote to a critic at the time, Rousseau explained that the picture represented the dream of the woman on the couch, on another occasion he declared that the couch was present only because he felt the painting needed just that touch of dark red.

Rousseau never traveled outside France or saw an actual jungle; his flora and fauna were based on illustrations in books and magazines and observations made on visits to botanical gardens and the zoo. Setting down each detail with painstaking fidelity and subtle nuances of color, and combining the imagined jungle with the "real" figure on the couch, Rousseau created in *The Dream,* his last picture, the culminating masterpiece of his career.

WIFREDO LAM. Cuban, born 1902. Also active in Spain, France, and Italy from 1923. Lives in Paris. *The Jungle.* 1943. Gouache on paper mounted on canvas, 7 feet 10¼ inches x 7 feet 6½ inches. Inter-American Fund. [140.45]

Lam's painting, like Rousseau's *Dream,* presents a night scene in the jungle, filled with a large number of forms crowded into the foreground plane. The atmosphere of the two works, however, is entirely different. Instead of the serenity of Yadwigha's dream, Lam depicts a terrifying vision, with intimations of savage magical rites. James Johnson Sweeney has described it: "Here, recollections or suggestions of some phantasmagoric jungle ritual set the theme of terror. Tree trunks that seem to flow into gigantic animal legs strike the rhythm of the composition, which is punctuated by cruel blade-like forms—actual instruments or palm leaves that echo them in shape. . . . Human and animal figures flow in and out this jungle warp, the human suddenly becoming animal, the animal turning human, and both in the end fixing themselves in our visual memory as masks, the paraphernalia of some nightmare sacrifice."

Rousseau's concept of the jungle was the imaginative projection of a petit bourgeois. Lam's was based much more closely on actual experience. Born in Cuba, he was the son of a Chinese businessman who had emigrated from Canton and a mother of mixed African, Indian, and European origin. Lam studied art first in Havana and then Madrid, remaining in Spain until the end of the Spanish Civil War, when he took refuge in France. In Paris, he met Picasso, who aided and encouraged him; and he became a member of the Surrealist group. He came back to Cuba at the outbreak of the Second World War, visited Haiti, and began to make more explicit use of Antillean subject matter, as in *The Jungle.* This tendency has persisted in his work even after his return to Europe in 1946.

The masklike faces in this picture recall some of Picasso's distortions (as for example in *Les Demoiselles d'Avignon,* page 47) and the primitive sculpture that inspired them. Lam, however, has given these forms a highly personal expression and has also imparted to the painting a coherent, though mysterious and Surrealist, context that is characteristic of his art.

81

RUFINO TAMAYO. Mexican, born 1899. Worked in New York, 1935–1948; in Paris 1949–1954. *Animals.* 1941. Oil on canvas, 30⅛ x 40 inches. Inter-American Fund. [165.42]

Against a lurid background of yellow and red, two ferocious beasts raise their heads and howl. On the barren ground at the left stands a large rock, and in the foreground lie three bare bones. Out of these simple elements Tamayo has created a terrifying image, all the more powerful because of its unnaturalistic color. The bared fangs, bristling muzzles, balefully glaring eyes, sharply pointed ears and tail, and upraised paw with extended claws all evoke fear. These do not seem to be specific animals in any actual moment of time but symbolic incarnations arousing our primordial dread.

Born in Oaxaca of Zapotec Indian stock, Tamayo came to maturity when the Mexican Revolution was finding expression in art through the activities of muralists such as Siqueiros, Orozco, and Rivera (see page 110) and through archaeological projects sponsored by the government, which revived interest in the indigenous pre-Columbian culture. At the age of twenty-two, Tamayo was appointed head of the Department of Ethnographic Drawing in the National Museum of Archaeology, where he came to know thoroughly the sculpture of the Aztecs, Mayans, and Toltecs. In the late 'twenties, he made the first of his periodic visits to the United States and, beginning in 1938, divided his time between Mexico and New York, where he taught during the winter. His encounter with the art of Picasso, which he saw in strength in The Museum of Modern Art's retrospective exhibition of 1939, was particularly crucial for his development and led him to adopt certain exaggerations and distortions of form for the sake of intensified emotion.

In his monograph on Tamayo, Robert Goldwater wrote: "His power lies in his ability to fuse naturally the most primitive and the most sophisticated. . . . By a fortunate chance of birth Tamayo grew up in the midst of a primitive culture and a folk tradition. By happy circumstances he was thrown, during his formative years, into the birth struggles of a modern style based in part upon the tradition he knew. And by his own artistic intelligence and sensibility he has assimilated some of the most advanced of contemporary artistic expression. . . . Yet he has remained close to the first sources of his art, and at his best has preserved the primitive immediacy with which it began."

JACKSON POLLOCK. American, 1912–1956. *The She-Wolf.* 1943. Oil, gouache, and plaster on canvas, 41⅞ x 67 inches. Purchase. [82.44]

Tamayo's beasts stand out with stark clarity against their background, but it is only with difficulty that we descry Pollock's she-wolf amid what at first appears to be a purely abstract network of thick calligraphic strokes filling the entire surface of the canvas. Heavily outlined in black, with strong white highlights, the creature advances to the left. Her body is overlaid with lines, curves, and patches of paint that do not serve to model her body in any conventional manner, and the forms within the remaining areas are indecipherable.

The She-Wolf is one of the first paintings in which Pollock achieved a personal means of expression. Previously, he had undergone a succession of influences, which included that of his teacher Thomas Hart Benton, Picasso's late-Cubist, decorative patterning, the dramatic content of the Mexican muralists, and the Surrealists' tapping of the subconscious as a source for imagery—fortified by Pollock's own undergoing of Jungian psychoanalysis. In this picture, Pollock seems to be striving for an amalgam of accepted mythology (the subject perhaps being identifiable as the foster-mother of Romulus and Remus, the founders of Rome) and a private iconography based on images dredged from his own unconscious. In 1944, Pollock said: "*She-Wolf* came into existence because I had to paint it. Any attempt on my part to say something about it, to attempt explanation of the inexplicable, could only destroy it."

Included in Pollock's first one-man show in 1943, *The She-Wolf* was bought by The Museum of Modern Art in the following year—the first of his works to enter into a museum collection. In its vigorous rhythms and filling of the entire surface with forceful strokes, it already anticipates the allover patterning that, from 1946 on, evolved in such classic "drip" paintings as his *One* (page 139).

GIORGIO DE CHIRICO. Italian, born Greece. 1888–1978. In Germany 1906; to Italy 1909. Worked in Paris 1911–1915, 1925–1939. *The Nostalgia of the Infinite.* 1913–1914 (dated on painting 1911). Oil on canvas, 53¼ x 25½ inches. Purchase. [87.36]

At a time when modern painters were attempting to portray reality in new ways, and when many of them, to assert the actuality of the picture's existence, were emphasizing flatness at the expense of illusionistic space, de Chirico set quite different goals for his art. He spoke of "the enigma of sudden revelation . . . things appear to us and awaken in us unknown sensations of joy and surprise; the sensations of revelation." He conveyed these sensations by reverting to the deep, linear perspective originated by fifteenth-century Italian artists and by filling his "metaphysical" pictures with elements based on the architecture and open squares of Italian cities. The "metaphysical" painting originated by de Chirico and a few associates in Italy was a repudiation of everything for which the Futurists had stood (see page 54). As Alfred H. Barr, Jr. has noted: "To the Futurists' concern with motion and the dynamics of the modern industrial age, the 'metaphysical' painters opposed an art of philosophical reverie, uncanny quiet, static incongruity, evoking a sense of mystery by assembling mysterious objects in strange settings." These concepts were later to prove highly influential for the Surrealists.

De Chirico had been living in Paris for several years when he painted *The Nostalgia of the Infinite;* its poetic title may reflect his homesickness for Italy. At the right of the picture, an arcade overshadows the dark foreground and a cubical object in the lower right corner. "The Roman arcade is a fatality," de Chirico wrote. "Its voice speaks in enigmas filled with a strangely Roman poetry. . . . In Rome the sense of prophecy is somehow larger: a feeling of infinite and distant grandeur inhabits it . . . a reflection of the space of the infinite." In the sunlit area in the middle distance of the painting, the shadow of an unidentified presence offstage falls from the right, while in the center other elongated shadows are cast by two tiny figures. "There are more enigmas in the shadow of a man who walks in the sun than in all the religions of the past, present and future," declared de Chirico. The background is occupied by a huge tower that rises above the rounded ground line almost to the top of the canvas. Its domed top is adorned with fluttering pennants, and beyond it a strangely colored sky, more green than blue, looms over a hilly landscape.

Writing of this painting, James Thrall Soby noted: "If the *Nostalgia* evokes an extraordinarily dreamlike illusion of infinite space and quiet, we must not disregard the skillful plastic means through which the illusion has been achieved . . . a quite abstract handling of form, testifying to the atavistic impetus of the artist's Renaissance heritage."

SALVADOR DALI. Spanish, born 1904. Active in Paris and New York. *The Persistence of Memory.* 1931. Oil on canvas, 9½ x 13 inches. Anonymous gift. [162.34]

The title of this painting is particularly apt, for Dali's limp watches have become among the most memorable invented images of our day; once seen, they stamp themselves indelibly upon the mind. "My whole ambition in the pictorial domain," he declared in his book *Conquest of the Irrational,* "is to materialize the images of concrete irrationality with the most imperialist fury of precision." To this end, he aped the meticulous technique of the nineteenth-century French painter Meissonier, producing what he called "hand-painted dream photographs." This verisimilitude gives Dali's fantastic visions the gripping credibility of our most vivid dreams—they are super-real. Like many other Surrealists, Dali was influenced by de Chirico's mysterious pictures, such as *The Nostalgia of the Infinite* (page 85), and especially by their evocative use of deep spatial perspective, which has the effect of detaching the figures and objects represented from everyday reality.

The small size of *The Persistence of Memory* (it measures less than this open book) concentrates its impact. Beyond stating that there may be some influence from Einstein's theory of relativity, Dali has given almost no clues to the interpretation of this picture, leaving us free to speculate on its meaning. The watches become limp, much as Alice's looking-glass dissolves. The landscape is barren and uninhabited, the sole tree dead, the rocky cliffs without vegetation. The only living creatures in this wasteland are the ants and the fly. Surprisingly, they attack the inorganic watches rather than what, at first, seems to be the carrion of some strange beast in the central foreground, but which on closer inspection proves to be a caricaturelike, profile self-portrait of Dali, with eyes closed in sleep or death.

Perhaps we have here a distant echo of a theme found in paintings and sculptures of earlier centuries, in which man is portrayed as a mortal being subject, with time, to death's corruption. In *The Persistence of Memory,* however, it is the instruments of time itself—the watches that measure it—which lose their durability and become vulnerable to scavenging attacks.

MAX ERNST. French, born Germany. 1891–1976. To France 1922; in U.S.A. 1941–1950. *Two Children Are Threatened by a Nightingale.* 1924. Oil on wood with wood construction, 27½ x 22½ x 4½ inches. Purchase. [256.37]

Even more, perhaps, than de Chirico or Dali, Ernst manifests in his art a total commitment to the irrational and a desire to go "beyond painting" by expressing in plastic terms poetic images that, welling up from the unconscious, have the force of revelation. In autobiographical notes published in 1942, he recounted an experience he had when bedridden with measles at the age of six: "A fever-vision provoked by an imitation-mahogany panel opposite his bed, the grooves of the wood taking successively the aspect of an eye, a nose, a bird's head, a *menacing nightingale,* a spinning top, and so on. Certainly little Max took pleasure in being afraid of these visions and later delivered himself voluntarily to provoke hallucinations of the same kind. . . . Possibly, the 'Two Children frightened by a Nightingale' have some connection with the fever-vision of 1897." Ernst also recalled that several days before executing this work, he had written a prose-poem beginning, "At nightfall, at the outskirts of the village, two children are threatened by a nightingale," and though he did not try to make an illustration for the poem, it nevertheless came out that way.

Birds have always played a large part in Ernst's personal iconography. Here, the nightingale—perhaps a symbol for seduction—appears in the sky at the left. One young girl attempts to fend it off with a knife, the other falls in a swoon. To the right, a faceless man bearing a small female form (the soul of the lifeless girl on the ground?) alights on the roof of a shack and reaches toward a protruding knob, perhaps to open the portal to some mysterious beyond.

In this brightly colored painting with its molded frame, we have deep space receding *into* the picture, and also, by the application of solid elements to the panel, space opening out *toward* the spectator. The three-dimensional components appeal to our touch as well as to our sight, so that, despite the diminutive size of the work and its figures, we feel ourselves drawn into the artist's fantasy.

JEAN (HANS) ARP. French, born Alsace (then part of Germany). 1887–1966. Lived in Switzerland 1959–1966. *Mountain, Table, Anchors, Navel.* 1925. Oil on cardboard with cutouts, 29⅝ x 23½ inches. Purchase. [77.36]

Early in his career, Arp made Cubist-inspired, geometrical abstractions but soon discovered his true bent lay in creating freely curving, "biomorphic" shapes that suggest, rather than imitate, organisms found in nature. A poet as well as an artist, he was readily attracted to antirational movements—first Dada, which came into being during the First World War and, in his words, "aimed to destroy the reasonable deceptions of man and recover the natural and unreasonable order," and later Surrealism, which took shape as a successor to Dada between 1922 and 1924. Arp's best-known statement about art, probably written in the 'twenties, was first published in 1932 and printed entirely without capitals and almost without punctuation. In it, he declared: "art is a fruit growing out of man like the fruit out of a plant like the child out of the mother. while the fruit of the plant grows independent forms and never resembles a balloon or a president in a cutaway suit the artistic fruit of man shows for the most part a ridiculous resemblance to the appearance of other things. reason tells man to stand above nature and to be the measure of all things. thus man thinks he is able to live and to create against the laws of nature and he creates abortions."

The *Mountain, Table, Anchors, Navel* dates from the time of Arp's close involvement with the Surrealists, who encouraged him to "ferret out the dream, the idea behind my plastic work, and to give it a name." Engaged in this quest for interpretation, Arp gave his works titles as poetic as they are irrational. He informs us: "These titles were often abbreviated little stories such as this for 'Mountain-Table-Anchors-Navel': 'A dreamer can make eggs as big as houses dance, bundle up flashes of lightning, and make an enormous mountain, dreaming of a navel and two anchors, hover over a poor enfeebled table that looks like the mummy of a goat.'" The navel, which appears in many of Arp's plastic works and poems, seems to have had a particular cosmic significance for him, at times denoting the generative forces of nature, at other times the sun, or the passage of time as measured by the face of a clock.

The technique of the *Mountain, Table, Anchors, Navel* might be regarded as a translation into two dimensions of the painted wood reliefs that Arp had begun to make in 1916. On the other hand, the cutouts, one of Arp's many formal inventions, might also be thought of as a variant of his collages, with shapes excised rather than pasted on. Since, like other Surrealists, he was sometimes interested in introducing automatism and the laws of chance into his compositions, it is worth noting that the open spaces allow for the possibility of changing the aspect of this work by altering the background against which it is set—black instead of white, for example.

JOAN MIRÓ. Spanish, born 1893. In Paris 1919–1940.
Painting. 1933. Oil on canvas, 68½ x 6 feet 5¼ inches.
Gift of the Advisory Committee. [229.37]

Like Arp's *Mountain, Table, Anchors, Navel,* Miró's
Painting is composed of abstract biomorphic forms.
Though it was actually developed from a collage made
in the same year, in which Miró had pasted onto a sheet
of paper nine halftone illustrations of machinery, he
characteristically metamorphosed the mechanical shapes
so that they seem to refer in highly schematized fashion
to animals, such as horned cattle. All the elements except
the one at the upper left, which is shaded and highlighted
in a manner that suggests three dimensions, are evenly
painted in black, white, or red, or rendered simply in
outline. The device of changing the tone of a shape as

it intersects another one appears frequently in Miró's
work from about this time on. He seems to have adopted
it as a convention to imply, within his overall two-
dimensional scheme, that the shapes should be thought
of as occupying different planes.

The biomorphic forms in the *Painting* float against a luminous, atmospheric background divided into geometrical fields of color. The smoky tones and blurred edges of
these areas are somewhat unusual for Miró, who in general prefers bright colors and crisp outlines. The large
size of the canvas and its resulting monumental effect are
also rather exceptional in his work, though in the following year he produced a series of big pictures intended to
serve as designs for tapestries, and later in his career he
created murals and large-scale ceramics to be placed in
architectural settings.

89

JOAN MIRÓ. Spanish, born 1893. In Paris 1919–1940. *The Hunter (Catalan Landscape)*. 1923–1924. Oil on canvas, 25½ x 39½ inches. Purchase. [95.36]

In *The Hunter (Catalan Landscape)*, which dates a decade before his *Painting* (page 89), Miró freely combined biomorphic and geometric shapes with calligraphic motifs to create a composition that also, at first glance, seems abstract. Actually, each element in this picture is a kind of visual shorthand, symbolically representing something in nature. Every detail can be precisely identified, thanks to annotations that Miró provided a quarter century later and subsequently amplified in conversation. This interpretation adds to our enjoyment of his whimsical humor, just as we can derive amusement from knowing how he transformed the elements of a seventeenth-century Dutch genre picture into his *Dutch Interior* (page 72). But even without deciphering *The Hunter,* we can appreciate the skill with which Miró deployed his black and colored motifs against the terracotta and yellow background to create a flat, decorative design.

The yellow area in the upper half of the picture represents both the Mediterranean and the sky, the rayed object in the upper center being the sun. In the left corner, an airplane on the Toulouse–Rabat route bears the flags of France and Miró's native Catalonia; just above it to the right is a star and a rainbow. In the opposite corner is a little boat flying the Spanish flag; nearby, seagulls hover over the waves.

On the terracotta shore, the stick figure at the left is the principal character, the hunter, who with cap, moustache, and beard stands smoking a pipe. He holds a gun in one hand, a rabbit in the other. To the right is a large eye, and beside it a carob tree and leaf, with other landscape elements on the ground nearby. In the foreground, from left to right, appear a vine, a skeletal sardine, a grill and flame for cooking the hunter's lunch, and the letters SARD, standing for "sardine."

Miró recalls that at the time he painted *The Hunter*, he was nearly starving and used in his compositions drawings into which he put the hallucinations provoked by his hunger. He had also recently come into close contact with the Surrealists, whose influence encouraged him, as it had Arp (page 88), to "go beyond Cubist form to attain poetry" and develop in his painting his predilection for fantasy and wit.

MATTA (Sebastian Antonio Matta Echaurren). Chilean, born 1912. In U.S.A. 1939–1948. Lives in Paris. *Le Vertige d'Éros.* 1944. Oil on canvas, 6 feet 5 inches x 8 feet 3 inches. Anonymous gift. [65.44]

Painted twenty years after Miró's *Hunter,* and by an artist of the succeeding generation, Matta's *Vertige d'Éros* represents not only a later phase of Surrealism but also a different tradition within that tendency. Miró's picture is flat, whereas Matta uses conventional modeling in the round and the deep illusionistic space encountered in de Chirico, Dali, and Ernst (pages 85–87). Miró's color is pure and generally light; Matta's is predominantly dark. Black washes are overlaid on the pigments beneath and partly rubbed away, so that the resulting gradations of shading produce an effect of atmospheric space. A network of lines is then superimposed to particularize this vague space by means of linear perspective.

Matta has said that the title of this work derives from Freud's statement that the life spirit, Eros, constantly challenged by the death instinct, Thanatos, induces in most people a sense of vertigo that they must continually combat in order to achieve a state of equilibrium. But when Matta told a friend that the name of the painting was *Le Vertige d'Éros,* she repeated it as *Les verts tiges des roses* ("the green stems of roses")—inadvertently making just such a pun as delighted the Surrealists.

This large painting depicts a subjective, psychological landscape of the mind, rather than an actual scene. There is no horizon line, so that the forms seem suspended within dimly lit space. As described by William Rubin: "The central metaphor . . . is that of infinite space which suggests simultaneously the cosmos and the recesses of the mind. Afloat in a mystical world of half-light that seems to emerge from unfathomable depths, a nameless morphology of shapes suggesting liquid, fire, roots, and sexual organs stimulates the awareness of our inner consciousness as it is when we trap it in reverie and dreams. . . . Matta invents new symbolic shapes." This new language of forms, he continues, "reaches back beyond dream activity to the more latent sources of psychic life: an iconography of consciousness as its exists before being hatched into the recognizable coordinates of everyday experience."

YVES TANGUY. American, born France. 1900–1955. To U.S.A. 1939. *Multiplication of the Arcs*. 1954. Oil on canvas, 40 x 60 inches. Mrs. Simon Guggenheim Fund. [559.54]

With its clearly modeled forms set in deep, illusionistically rendered space, the *Multiplication of the Arcs* is a landscape within the tradition of Surrealism's precursor de Chirico (page 85), whose work first inspired Tanguy to become a painter. Instead of de Chirico's empty, open areas, however, the entire lower half of this canvas is densely crowded with pebbles, boulders, and bonelike shapes, interspersed with large shafts of granite. In James Thrall Soby's words, "The picture is a sort of boneyard of the world, its inexplicable objects gathered in fantastic profusion before a soft and brooding sky."

This painting, Tanguy's last major work, is the consummate expression of his lifelong preoccupation with strange rock formations. During his childhood, he spent his vacations at his family's house in Locronan, in the Finistère region of Brittany, and he seems always to have retained a vivid impression of its rocky shore and of the Stone Age menhirs and dolmens that abound in the nearby fields. The curious bastionlike tablelands that he saw on a trip to Africa so fascinated him that he incorporated their shapes into several paintings of the early 'thirties. In 1939, he traveled across the United States and was especially struck by the geological phenomena of the Southwest.

The title of the picture, *Multiplication of the Arcs*, indicates that Tanguy's interest in rocks led him to acquire some familiarity with geology and its terminology. "Island arcs" are curving chains of islands, such as the Aleutians or the Antilles, found off the shores of continents; "mountain arcs" are the similarly curved systems of mountains that rim the coasts inland. Behind these primary festoons of mountains there may arise secondary arcs, such as the Canadian Rockies, formed by deposits washed inward from the coastal ranges. According to one theory of geophysics, continents were born by the slow accretion of materials resulting from the eruption of undersea volcanoes and extruded from the ocean, together with sedimentary rocks continually added at the margins of the land.

Tanguy's *Multiplication of the Arcs* would seem to be an artist's, rather than a scientist's, vision of a process that took place billions of years ago. In true Surrealist fashion, he has accentuated the forms of the spherical pebbles with parti-colored layers, so frequently found on beaches, to make them resemble eyes. In like fashion, he has given the row of rocks rising up along the horizon under a lowering sky the aspect of menacing presences.

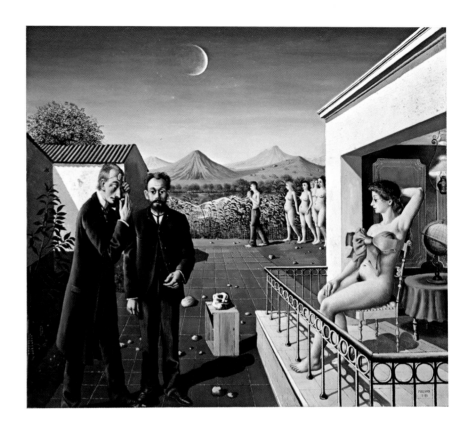

PAUL DELVAUX. Belgian, born 1897. *Phases of the Moon.* 1939. Oil on canvas, 55 x 63 inches. Purchase. [504.51]

Like Tanguy, Delvaux was influenced by de Chirico, and by the Surrealists, though never formally an adherent of their movement. He creates a world in which illogically juxtaposed dramatis personae move like sleepwalkers through inexplicable situations that seem to occasion them no surprise. At one time or another, almost everyone has dreamed of finding himself in public with no clothes on, but Delvaux's figures accept this predicament without embarrassment. All his characters, in fact, whether clothed or naked, are generally too self-engrossed to be aware of anyone else.

Delvaux derived the man in the frock coat at the left of the *Phases of the Moon* from an engraving by Édouard Riou illustrating a late-nineteenth-century edition of Jules Verne's *Journey to the Center of the Earth.* He represents the central character of that tale, the narrator's uncle, a German professor of "philosophy, chemistry, geology, mineralogy, and many other ologies." Delvaux has said that, as a child, he was so fascinated by this illustration that he made a copy of it to hang in his study. Years later, he recalled the figure and decided to incor-

porate it into a painting, selecting the subject of the moon's phases as appropriate to the scholar's scientific vocation. To counteract the figure's austerity, he placed him in an alien, disquieting setting peopled with nudes. The landscape background with its conical mountains may refer indirectly to Verne's novel, which was inspired by accounts of a scientist's descent into the flaming crater of Stromboli, though in the book the locale was moved to Iceland. The lighting of the scene is ambiguous. Is it day or night? Within a star-filled sky, the right side of the moon shines brightly; but lit from some unseen source at the left, all objects cast shadows that fall to the right.

Gazing with myopic intensity at the object in his hands, the learned man conforms to Verne's description of a savant who "was once known to classify six hundred different geological specimen by their weight, hardness, fusibility, sound, taste, and smell. . . . My uncle was fifty years old; tall, thin, and wiry. Large spectacles hid, to a certain extent, his vast, round, and goggle eyes, while his nose was irreverently compared to a thin file." This figure copied from Riou's engraving, who makes his first appearance in Delvaux's art in the *Phases of the Moon,* has continued to haunt the artist's fantasies for more than twenty years, recurring in a number of other pictures.

93

ODILON REDON. French, 1840–1916. *Silence.* c. 1911. Oil on gesso on paper, 21¼ x 21½ inches. Lillie P. Bliss Collection. [113.34]

Painted in monochromatic browns within an oval frame and set against a pale green background, this somber figure with hooded eyes has a secretive, otherworldly aspect. The picture's mood of melancholy reverie relates it to the literature of the Symbolists, with whom Redon was closely associated. The thin oil wash used as a medium contributes to the evanescent effect.

This is an evocative image and, at the same time, with its gesture of upraised fingers sealing the lips, a quite literal representation of silence. It is not only more explicit than many of Redon's paintings and prints but is also related to other renditions of the subject in Western art. Among the specific sources almost certainly known to Redon are Fra Angelico's fresco in the cloister of San Marco in Florence, showing St. Peter Martyr holding a finger to his lips to enjoin silence, and a marble relief known as *Le Silence,* by the nineteenth-century French sculptor Auguste Préault, on a tomb in the Père-Lachaise Cemetery in Paris. The relief shows the same gesture as the figure in Redon's painting and encloses the head in a similar way within an oval frame against a rectangular background.

Redon treated the subject of silence in several other works. Closest to this picture is a mural done at about the same time (1910–1911) as a decoration over the doorway to the library of his friend Gustave Fayet, occupying what had formerly been the cloister of the abandoned abbey of Fontfroide. These and other connections with the painting in The Museum of Modern Art have been discussed by Theodore Reff; he identifies the features as those of the artist's wife and suggests that, as she had recently been extremely ill, the *Silence* may be a personal expression of Redon's profound sadness and sense of the closeness of death.

RENÉ MAGRITTE. Belgian, 1898–1967. *The False Mirror.* 1928. Oil on canvas, 21¼ x 31⅞ inches. Purchase. [133.36]

Magritte was strongly influenced by de Chirico (page 85) and, like him, sought to reveal the hidden affinities linking objects that are normally dissociated. His pictures present a challenge to the "real" world by turning every-day logic topsy-turvy, substituting a different kind of order, which our unconscious mind recognizes as having a rationale of its own.

In *The False Mirror,* equivalences are established between the eye and the cloud-filled sky that forms its iris, the pupil being the black disk that floats like a sun in the center. Isolated from any anatomical reference to a depicted face, the huge eye not only fills the entire height and breadth of the canvas but also seems to extend beyond the picture's edge at left and right. The image owes much of its compelling effect to this inflated scale and to the meticulous finish with which it is painted, recalling works by the Flemish old masters of Magritte's native Belgium. In his adherence to illusionistic technique, Magritte anticipated the "hand-painted dream photographs" of his fellow Surrealist Dali (page 86).

In contradistinction to Redon, Magritte always insisted that his art could not be equated with symbolism, for this would imply a supremacy of the invisible over the visible. "My paintings have no reducible meaning: they *are* a meaning," he declared.

The title of this picture was given to it by Paul Nougé, a writer who was a member of the Surrealist group that Magritte helped to found in Brussels shortly before his sojourn in the environs of Paris, where *The False Mirror* was painted. Magritte's visualization of the mind's eye has become a kind of modern icon, frequently copied or adapted, as in the CBS trademark.

GIACOMO BALLA. Italian, 1871–1958. *Street Light.* 1909. Oil on canvas, 68¾ x 45¼ inches. Hillman Periodicals Fund. [7.54]

In *The Photographer's Eye,* John Szarkowski points out that by taking a fragment of the real world and isolating it from its context, the photographer could "claim for it some special significance, a meaning which went beyond simple description. The compelling clarity with which a photograph recorded the trivial suggested that the subject had never been properly seen, that it was in fact *not* trivial, but filled with undiscovered meaning. . . . Photographs could be read as symbols." In all likelihood, it was this perception by photographers that led modern paint-

ers to adopt the device of making a single object or detail the subject of a picture, as in the *Street Light.* We know, in fact, that Balla was interested in photography—though obviously from a technical standpoint this picture could hardly be further removed from camera work.

Electric street lights had only recently been installed in Rome and were generally regarded as unartistic when, in 1909, Balla was struck by seeing one in the Piazza Termini with "the moon in such a position that it gave the impression of being less luminous than the lamp." The motif appealed to him for two reasons. For several years, he had painted works in which light was the principal theme. Secondly, he was one of a number of dissident painters and poets who sought to free Italy from enslavement to the past by glorifying the dynamism of modern life and the new beauty of machines. Balla has said that the *Street Light* was "above all a demonstration that romantic moonlight had been surpassed by the light of the modern electric street lamp. This was the end of Romanticism in art. From my picture came the phrase 'Let's Kill the Moonlight!'" This was the title of a proclamation published later in the same year by the poet Tommaso Marinetti, who shortly before had issued the first manifesto of Futurism—a movement soon joined by the avant-garde artists, including Severini (page 43) and Boccioni (pages 54–55) as well as Balla.

The *Street Light* is painted in a technique derived from Seurat (page 17); but instead of dots of pigment, Balla has used brilliant chevrons. The rays of light are shown refracted into their component pure colors—of maximum intensity, rather than rainbow delicacy, carrying out his concept that the artificial illumination produced by a modern mechanism is far more powerful than the effects of nature. There is additional symbolism in the star shape placed at the core of the lamp. Dark, sketchily painted masses of foliage enframe Balla's striking image in curves reminiscent of Art Nouveau, the style that from the turn of the century until the rise of Futurism had epitomized "modernism" in Italy.

96

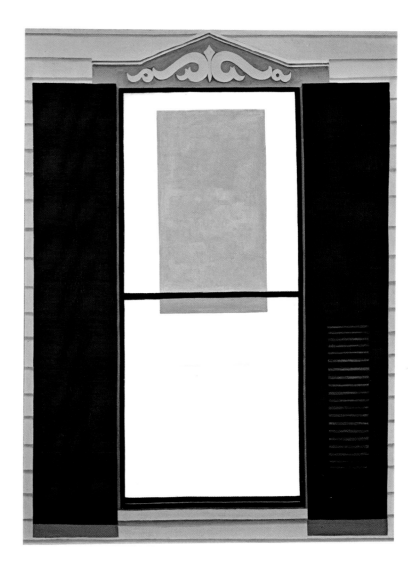

GEORGIA O'KEEFFE. American, born 1887. *Lake George Window.* 1929. Oil on canvas, 40 x 30 inches. Acquired through the Richard D. Brixey Bequest. [144.45]

Like Balla, O'Keeffe has taken a single motif from perceived reality and, by isolating it from its surroundings, intensified its visual and emotional impact. At first sight, her *Lake George Window* seems far closer to photography than his *Street Light;* and it is tempting to push the analogy to camera work, in view of the fact that O'Keeffe's art was first exhibited in 1916 at the famous avant-garde "291" gallery directed by the master photographer Alfred Stieglitz, whom she subsequently married. On closer inspection, however, what seems paramount in this painting is the rigid selectivity of O'Keeffe's approach, which is highly stylized, deleting any details that might mar the immaculate precision of the forms and the surface of the canvas. By contrast, a photograph of the same Lake George farmhouse by Stieglitz is more complex in composition and is taken at an angle, with a raking light to accentuate the textures of the clapboards.

O'Keeffe presents the structure in a strictly frontal, symmetrical view and drastically reduces its three-dimensionality. Commenting on this painting, Lloyd Goodrich says: "Though entirely realistic, its severe simplification, stark rectangular forms and austere color harmony, and the fine relations of all elements, give it the quality of a handsome abstract design."

97

PAUL KLEE. German, 1879–1940. Born and died in Switzerland. *Equals Infinity.* 1932. Oil on canvas mounted on wood, $20\frac{1}{4}$ x $26\frac{7}{8}$ inches. Acquired through the Lillie P. Bliss Bequest. [90.50]

Klee was a poetic philosopher engaged throughout his life in a continual quest for the pictorial means best suited to expressing the ultimate truths that transcend observed reality. "Art does not reproduce the visible; it renders visible" was one of his aphorisms. His efforts to perceive relationships between the animate and the inanimate, the individual and the cosmos, link him to the Romantic tradition; but he was in close contact with the chief currents of twentieth-century thought and was wholly modern in his commitment to nonrealistic modes of art.

"In the past," Klee wrote, "artists represented things they had seen on earth, things they liked seeing or might have liked to see. Today they reveal the relativity of visible things; they express their belief that the visible is only an isolated aspect in relation to the universe as a whole, and that other, invisible truths are the overriding factors. . . . Art is a parable of Creation. . . . All higher and still higher questions of form are vital factors in artistic communication; but they do not in themselves produce art of the highest level. For at that level, mystery begins and the intellect counts for nothing. At the highest level, imagination is guided by instinctual stimuli, and illusions are created which buoy us up and stir us more than do the familiar things of earth. . . . Art plays an unknowing game with things. Just as a child at play imitates us, so we at play imitate the forces which created and are creating the world."

Since Klee intended his art to communicate ideas, he gave great importance to his titles and almost always inscribed them on his works. *Equals Infinity* is more literal a title than most, being simply the expression in words of the two mathematical symbols in the center right of the painting. Significantly, however, the essential other half of the equation is not given, except as the entire picture implies it and leaves it open to our interpretation.

This is one of a group of paintings in which Klee was particularly concerned with portraying light-filled space through color. His adoption of small dots of pigment to achieve this effect recalls Seurat's technique (page 17); but, unlike Seurat, Klee was not attempting to describe visible data or the spatial perspective of nature. The fact that the dots are square instead of circular gives a clue to his source: the Early Christian and Byzantine mosaics that he had seen on several trips to the Italian mainland and Sicily. In such works, small, irregularly set squares of stone or glass—colored for the figures, gold for the background—capture the shimmer of light and convey an immaterial, spiritual world. But whereas in the mosaics all figures and objects represented are clearly recognizable, though stylized, in Klee's picture inchoate shapes seem to float like clouds or their reflections in water. Perhaps the tiny squares may be thought of as atoms, connoting a universe made up of an infinitude of particles that move in obedience to laws that man's mind, even when aided by intuition as well as by science, can only vaguely apprehend.

98

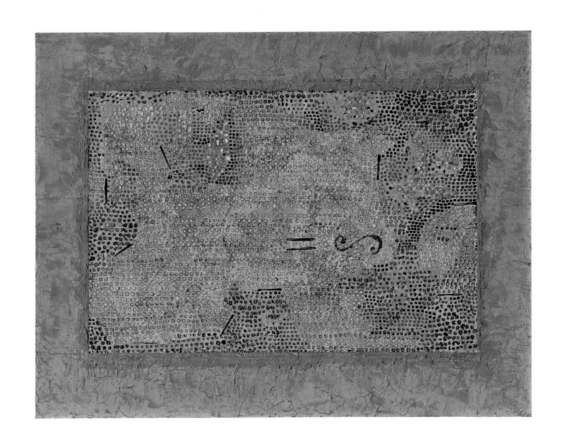

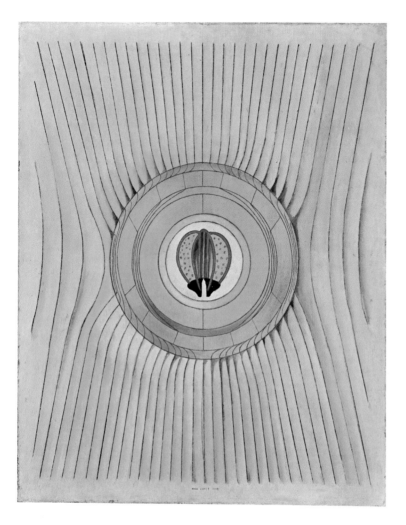

MAX ERNST. French, born Germany. 1891–1976. To France 1922; in U.S.A. 1941–1950. *The Blind Swimmer.* 1934. Oil on canvas, 36⅜ x 29 inches. Gift of Mrs. Pierre Matisse and Helena Rubinstein Fund. [228.68]

With its simplified forms and symmetrical composition, this painting has a strangely emblematic quality. Within the innermost of a series of concentric circles there lies quiescent an organism that resembles a seedpod, a larva, or one of the extinct Paleozoic marine invertebrates called trilobites. From the rims of the disks that surround it, lines extend outward in a pattern like ripples of water or the graining of wood. We sense here a metaphor for embryonic or primeval life and the secret workings of nature's creative forces.

The figure of speech "blind swimmer" recurs several times in Ernst's writings. For example, he describes his situation at an early stage in his life, between 1910 and 1911: "The young man, eager for knowledge, avoided any studies which might degenerate into breadwinning. Instead his pursuits were those considered futile by his professors—predominantly painting. Other futile pursuits: reading seditious philosophers and unorthodox poetry.... Attracted by the most audacious spirits, he was willing to receive the most contradictory influences.... What to do about consequent confusion? Struggle like a blind swimmer?"

Having decided that he wished his art to be one of revelation (see page 87), one memorable day in 1925 Ernst discovered a procedure that he called *frottage* ("rubbing"). By dropping pieces of paper at random on the floor and rubbing them with black lead, he obtained impressions of the wood's graining. Gazing intently at them, he found they intensified his visionary capacities. "By widening in this way the active part of the mind's hallucinatory faculties, I came to assist *as spectator* at the birth of all my works.... Blind swimmer, I have made myself see. *I have seen.* ... Enter, enter, have no fear of being blinded."

Thereafter, the images in Ernst's paintings appeared to him full blown. He records that early in 1934, "I met a blind swimmer" (referring either to this picture or another version of the same year). Thus, *The Blind Swimmer* may allude not only to the act of creation in general, but even more specifically to Ernst's attitude toward his own creativity.

JASPER JOHNS. American, born 1930. *Target with Four Faces.* 1955. Encaustic on newspaper over canvas, 26 x 26 inches, surmounted by four tinted plaster faces in wooden box with hinged front, 3¾ x 26 x 3 inches (open). Gift of Mr. and Mrs. Robert C. Scull. [8.58]

The *Target with Four Faces* has in common with Ernst's *Blind Swimmer* an emblematic quality, a symmetrical composition built around concentric circles, and a reference to sightlessness. These fortuitous resemblances apart, however, the two works are entirely different. Ernst's image, originating in a figure of speech, is intended to evoke poetic associations to a literary content. Johns's target, on the other hand, is a commonplace, man-made, universal object. He has said that selecting something already designed, something "the mind already knows," gave him "room to work on other levels"; and he also chose "objects so familiar that the spectator can cease to think about them and concentrate on the poetic qualities of the picture itself" as a painted object. Ernst's painting, whatever its ultimate relation to *frottage* or its suggestion of wood graining, has a smooth, even surface. Conversely, whereas one would expect a target to be given the flattest coat of paint possible, Johns has given his picture an uneven surface, using a complex medium of pigments mixed in melted wax and applied with broken brushstrokes over newspaper.

There are still other paradoxes in this work. Having chosen a flat subject and called attention to the picture's surface by varying its texture, Johns then placed above his target and its enclosing square four boxes containing three-dimensional plaster heads (not identical casts but differing slightly one from another), with their tops cut off at a point below the eyes. Furthermore, in looking at a target, one generally tends to focus on the bull's-eye; Johns has countered this tendency by giving the enframing square a strong red color and topping it by the orange-colored heads.

Despite the contradictory interpretations given to his paintings by critics, Johns has refused to admit that they have any latent significance. It is nevertheless impossible for the spectator to respond solely to the purely formal qualities in the *Target with Four Faces*. Inevitably, the target surmounted by four truncated, eyeless casts of a single face stimulates our associations and raises questions. What is meant by this strange juxtaposition? and what is the implication of the hinged top that can be lowered at will to enclose the row of heads and hide them from our view?

EDWIN DICKINSON. American, 1891–1978. *Composition with Still Life.* 1933–1937. Oil on canvas, 8 feet 1 inch x 6 feet 5¾ inches. Gift of Mr. and Mrs. Ansley W. Sawyer. [173.52]

This is the largest and one of the most mysterious pictures by Dickinson, whose work defies classification within any of the generally accepted categories of modern art. Perhaps what is most "modern" about him is the ambiguity of his paintings, in respect to both style and subject matter, and his refusal to require them to have any frame of reference other than their own visual raison d'être. He has explained his tilting of objects and use of unusual points of view as devices adopted to force the viewer to observe what is actually shown and react to it, instead of "coasting on the memory of previous experience"; in this, there is a certain analogy to Johns's intention (page 101).

In the *Composition with Still Life,* the overturned vases, the rose, the large auger, the outflung hand above them, and the sails at the top are rendered with almost academic precision. Other sections, including the stream and broken planking in the foreground, the ornate frame at the left, the bodies of the two nudes, and the background in the upper section of the canvas, are blurred and indistinct. The unnaturalistic lighting and strange color—chiefly white, gray, and blue, with touches of red and brown—add to the hallucinatory effect.

Dorothy C. Miller has written of Dickinson's pictures: "At first glance these complex paintings . . . suggest literary associations or a surrealist attitude. But closer study reveals that this is a completely visual world, dense with objects which, though not easy to identify, come out of exact and searching observation. With purely plastic means Dickinson plays with light and shade and perspective as boldly as the artists of the baroque, and this play he has complicated and enriched through discontinuity in the handling of form and color, here holding and defining forms in clear articulation by light and perspective, there arbitrarily tearing them with shadow and impinging objects, or drifting them away from anchored fact through clouds of paint that turn defining edges into mist and illusion."

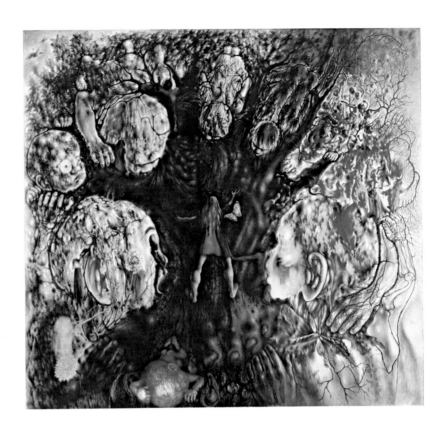

PAVEL TCHELITCHEW. American, born Russia. 1898–
1957. Worked in Western Europe and England from 1921.
In U.S.A. 1938–1952. *Hide-and-Seek.* 1940–1942. Oil on
canvas, 6 feet 6½ inches x 7 feet ¾ inch. Mrs. Simon
Guggenheim Fund. [344.42]

Unlike Dickinson's *Composition with Still Life,* Tchelitchew's *Hide-and-Seek* has a symbolic intent; in it, the
artist attempted to summarize his philosophical specula-
tions on the mystery of life. As Alfred H. Barr, Jr. has
said, in this intricate allegory "the tree of life becomes a
clock of the seasons; its greens and fiery reds and wintry
blues celebrate the annual cycle of death and rebirth."
The spiral form of its composition is one that Tchelitchew (like Leonardo da Vinci) recognized as basic to
motion in nature.

Tchelitchew shared with the Cubists the conviction
that our memory of something is as important as the aspect it presents to us at any one moment. He differed
from them, however, in wishing to portray the full sensuous appeal that things make to us. He also believed that
the Cubists erred in inclining toward two-dimensionality,
rather than expanding three-dimensionality to convey
the idea of the fourth dimension, time.

For Tchelitchew, metamorphosis—seeing one object
in another—was not only the key to perceiving an image
in its totality but was also the secret of poetry, without
which art cannot exist. In 1934, he sketched a gnarled oak
tree in a park in Sussex. He later wrote, "It took eight
years for this tree to grow and become *Hide-and-Seek.*"
The actual painting of the picture, in part through automatism, took three years. Through a sequence of drawings and studies (several owned by The Museum of
Modern Art), trees gradually metamorphosed into figures and parts of the body. It was Tchelitchew's theory
that such changes take place rhythmically in time. He
endeavored to show this vital principle by rendering
images as partially transparent and presenting them in
three perspectives: as seen at eye level, from above, and
from below. Color, too, he used symbolically to define
the human body and the four elements that compose the
physical universe. Thus, ocher signifies bones and the
earth; green, lymph and water; blue, arteries and veins,
and air; and cold yellow with a magenta halo, nerves and
fire. White symbolizes the glands. Even minor details in
the picture have significance—for example, the dande-
lions, in the lower left quadrant, were included because
of their "ephemeral existence and terrific tenacity."

103

Max Beckmann. German, 1884-1950. Worked in Amsterdam, 1936-1947; in U.S.A. 1947-1950. *Departure.* 1932-1933. Oil on canvas; triptych, center panel 7 feet ¾ inch x 45⅜ inches, side panels 7 feet ¾ inch x 39¼ inches. Anonymous gift. [6.42.1–3]

This large triptych presents an allegory with a highly personal symbolism that cannot be explained by traditional iconography. It was painted over the course of a year and a half, a period during which the Nazis came to power and Beckmann was dismissed as a "degenerate artist" from his professorship at a Frankfurt art academy. He said, nevertheless, that the *Departure* has no specifically tendentious meaning but could well be applicable to all times. The two side wings, both darker and more crowded than the panel they flank, are obviously an expression of brutality, repression, horror, and despair, in contrast to the brightness, openness, and calm conveyed by the central section.

Beckmann declared that he not only would not, but actually could not, unravel the painting's meaning: "The picture speaks to me of truths impossible for me to put into words and of which I did not ever know before. I can only speak to people who consciously or unconsciously, already carry within them a similar metaphysical code. Departure, yes departure, from the illusions of life to-

ward the essential realities that lie hidden beyond. . . ."

Notwithstanding Beckmann's statement, many attempts have been made to interpret the details of this triptych. The central panel (which in his notebooks he called "the Homecoming") is probably the easiest to decipher. The child, an embodiment of love and hope for the future, is borne by a woman who wears a peaked Phrygian cap, a conventional emblem of freedom. The veiled figure at the left holds a fish—not only the age-old Christian symbol of redemption but also an image that Beckmann had used in earlier paintings to signify virility. The crowned figure at the right turns his back on the past and with upraised right hand faces resolutely toward the

open sea, which will bear the voyagers to their unknown future. Lilly von Schnitzler, a friend and patron of Beckmann's, recalls that he told her in 1937: "The King and Queen have freed themselves of the tortures of life—they have overcome them. The Queen carries the greatest treasure—Freedom—as her child in her lap. Freedom is the one thing that matters—it is the departure, the new start."

Beyond this, we are left to experience for ourselves the power inherent in this work. Its richness of allusion, unexpected combination of striking images, and ambiguity are all characteristic of many modern expressions in literature and the film, as well as in the plastic arts.

Peter Blume. American, born Russia 1906. To U.S.A. 1911. *The Eternal City.* 1934–1937. Oil on composition board, 34 x 47⅞ inches. Mrs. Simon Guggenheim Fund. [574.42]

Though not completed until 1937, this picture had its origins in impressions dating from 1932–1933—the same year in which Beckmann painted his *Departure* (pages 104–105). *The Eternal City* is a synthesis of images seen, and ideas generated, during the months that Blume spent on a fellowship in Italy, at a time when the Fascist dictatorship was at its height. The scowling jack-in-the-box head of Mussolini was, in fact, inspired by a papier-mâché sculpture of Il Duce on view at the Tenth Anniversary celebration of Fascist domination. Although Blume found this head with its strident red, yellow, and green a discordant element, he decided to interpolate it nevertheless, because other considerations seemed to him to be more compelling than the picture's aesthetic harmony.

The themes incorporated in the composition were developed in a series of painstakingly elaborated studies. The fragments of sculpture in the foreground, the sub-

terranean passages beyond, the curved building at the right, and the ruins in the background are an archaeological medley of views of the Catacombs, the Forum, and the Colosseum. The lighted shrine at the left Blume saw in the church of San Marco in Florence, where he was struck by the incongruity of this statue of the Man of Sorrows bedecked with such symbols of human vanity and power as jewels, swords, and military epaulets. The crippled beggar woman in front of the shrine is of a type that Blume might have encountered all too frequently. Directly under the head of Mussolini are grinning caricatures of a capitalist and a Black Shirt thug; beyond, in the sunlit Forum, foot soldiers and cavalry are surrounded by people crawling on the ground.

As an allegory, *The Eternal City* is far more topical in its references to a particular time and place than is the *Departure* and is composed of more readily identifiable details, though its implications transcend these specific allusions. It also differs from Beckmann's painting in the meticulous finish of its technique. This was influenced by the works of Flemish and Italian old masters that Blume saw while abroad; it likewise parallels, to some extent, Dali's super-realism (page 86).

FRANCIS BACON. British, born 1909. *Painting.* 1946. Oil and tempera on canvas, 6 feet 5⅞ inches x 52 inches. Purchase. [229.48]

Bacon, like Blume, portrays a dictator, who seems all the more menacing because he is unidentified and, with the upper part of his face concealed, unidentifiable, though the mouth and jutting jaw vaguely resemble news photographs of Mussolini. The title *Painting* gives no hint of any specific person or situation. As in a nightmare or Kafka's novel *The Castle,* this very anonymity and our inability to define or explain just what is taking place aggravate the sense of horror.

Beneath an umbrella set like a baldachin that shields his face with deep shadow, the monstrous figure sits on a rostrum surrounded by microphones. The chrome tubes of the circular railing run like spits through sides of beef, while behind him a huge butchered carcass, split open, assumes the form of a crucified figure. Drawn window shades shut out any world beyond this charnel house. The dissonant reds, purples, and prominent blacks intensify the atmosphere of violence and dread.

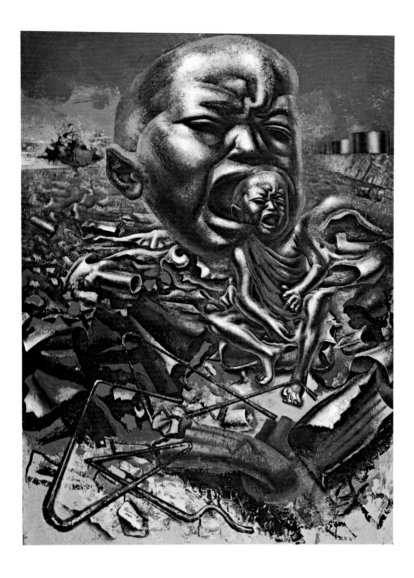

DAVID ALFARO SIQUEIROS. Mexican, 1896–1974. *Echo of a Scream.* 1937. Duco on wood, 48 x 36 inches. Gift of Edward M. M. Warburg. [633.39]

Siqueiros focuses on the victims, rather than the perpetrators, of brutality. Though the *Echo of a Scream* was inspired by the Spanish Civil War, in which he was a combatant, he has termed it a more general "cry to all human beings to avoid wars."

Behind the desolate, wailing baby—the only living creature in a wasteland devoid of vegetation and heaped with rubble, broken cannons, and twisted metal—rises an apparition of the infant's head, monstrously enlarged. The suffering of one human being is magnified to denote the agony of a multitude. The color, with its leaden grays, browns, and blood red, is symbolic in its own right.

Like Bacon (page 107) and many other modern artists, Siqueiros collected photographs and reproductions taken from books and periodicals, which provided him with a store of visual motifs that were frequently completely transformed from their original context. In this case, the source for Siqueiros' compelling central image was a detail taken from an illustration in a 1925 issue of the *National Geographic,* demonstrating the way in which women in Kenya carry their babies on their backs.

Siqueiros is prototypical of the engaged artist; his commitment to his political beliefs caused him to be imprisoned several times.

JACK LEVINE. American, born 1915. *Election Night.* 1954. Oil on canvas, 63⅛ inches x 6 feet ½ inch. Gift of Joseph H. Hirshhorn. [153.55]

Levine's comment on one aspect of the political process in America focuses on no particular election, party, or individual but satirizes a common phenomenon of our national life. He is an astute reporter, and his types are sharply observed.

The complacent figure in the center can be identified as the successful candidate. He is surrounded by those who, having helped in bringing him to power, now obviously expect to profit by sharing in the spoils of victory. The lantern-jawed man embracing him while ogling the cigarette girl appears to be a professional politico, while the sharp-nosed, distinguished-looking gentleman in the right foreground, apparently as oblivious of his surroundings as of the disarray of his attire, seems to typify a capitalist banker. All the personages seated around the table seem equally alienated from one another, either sunk in self-absorption or, bored with their companions, letting their attention stray beyond their own circle.

Levine draws a distinction between expressionistic representation, which he considers too subjective a reflection of the artist's own reaction, and what he terms "distortion for empathy," which leads him to adopt a canon for his figures that gives them disproportionately large heads. He explains: "You give something a larger area because it is more important. . . . You distort for editorial reasons—a dignified way of saying caricature. . . . Distortion is always a dramatic vehicle." Another hallmark of Levine's style is clear focus that is partially blurred by glazes of semitransparent oil paint, applied in a technique like that of Titian and Rubens.

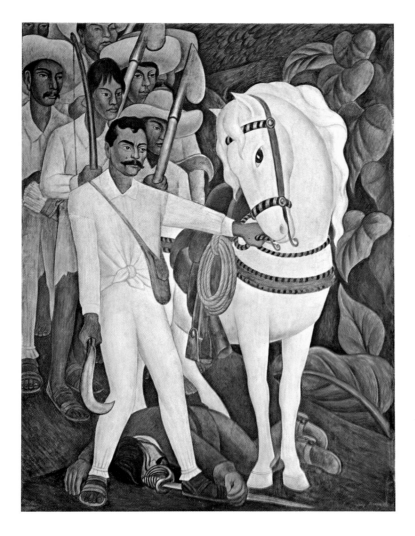

DIEGO RIVERA. Mexican, 1886–1957. Worked in Europe 1907–1921. In U.S.A. 1930–1933, 1940. *Agrarian Leader Zapata.* 1931. Fresco, 7 feet 9¾ inches x 6 feet 2 inches. Abby Aldrich Rockefeller Fund. [1631.40]

The art of fresco—painting a mural on moist plaster with pigments that are incorporated into the plaster as it dries—was common in Italy during the late Middle Ages and early Renaissance for the decoration of churches and civic buildings. It was revived in Mexico in modern times, when a group of artists saw its value for social propaganda to educate the people in the aims and achievements of the recently concluded Revolution. During the 'twenties and 'thirties, public buildings throughout Mexico were adorned with frescoes that emphasized the glorious pre-Columbian civilization, the Spanish Conquest, the oppression of the Indians, the domination of the populace by the clergy during the colonial period, the subsequent exploitation of Mexico by foreign capitalists (especially those from the United States), and the heroic struggle that began in 1910 and ended with the firm establishment of the revolutionary régime in 1920.

Rivera was one of the principal artists engaged in these vast government-sponsored mural projects. The *Agrarian Leader Zapata* is the replica of a portion of one of the panels he painted in 1930 in the Palace of Cortés, Cuernavaca, in which, accepting anachronism for the sake of symbolism, he portrayed Zapata holding Cortés's stallion. Emiliano Zapata was among the earliest agitators for social and agrarian reforms, but during the internecine strife of the Revolution, he opposed one of the other leaders, Carranza, who became head of the government in 1915. After seeking for several years to gain control by guerilla warfare, Zapata was killed by Carranza's forces in 1919.

There is little reflection of such a bloody and agitated history in this static composition, one of seven frescoes commissioned in 1931 for an exhibition of Rivera's work at The Museum of Modern Art. The knife Zapata carries is of a type used for cutting sugar cane, and he and the figures behind him wear the regional costumes of the State of Morelos, in which Cuernavaca is located. The horse, however, has another, more distant derivation. It is based on paintings by the fifteenth-century Florentine Paolo Uccello, whose works Rivera had studied during a long sojourn in Europe from 1904 to 1921. In the latter year, he returned to Mexico and became active in the ranks of the revolutionary artists.

JOSÉ CLEMENTE OROZCO, Mexican, 1883–1949. In U.S.A. 1917–1918, 1927–1934, 1940, 1945–1946. *Zapatistas.* 1931. Oil on canvas, 45 x 55 inches. Anonymous gift. [470.37]

In this painting of the followers of the assassinated agrarian leader Zapata, there is no individual hero. A line of peons, followed by their womenfolk, press onward. The large figures of the mounted horsemen guarding them loom above them, and in the background mountains rise beneath a dark, cloud-filled sky. The composition is based on rhythmic repetitions: the forward inclination of the figures in the foreground, the almost identical frontal postures and sombreros of the first and third horsemen that alternate with those of the second and fourth. Except for the men's white shirts and pants and their yellow hats, the color is somber, with dark red predominating. This is in keeping with Orozco's tragic view of life. He saw the Mexican Revolution largely in terms of human suffering, including that caused by strife among the rival factions seeking to wrest power from one another.

Together with Rivera and Siqueiros (page 108), Orozco was one of the great triumvirate of Mexican artists who revived the art of fresco. Though the *Zapatistas* is an easel painting, it is closely related in style and theme to frescoes Orozco did in Mexico, especially those for the National Preparatory School in the capital. This picture, however, was painted in New York during Orozco's second sojourn in the United States. Among the frescoes that he executed in this country are those at Pomona College in California, the New School for Social Research in New York, and Dartmouth College in Hanover, New Hampshire; as well as the *Dive Bomber and Tank,* a portable mural with six interchangeable parts commissioned by The Museum of Modern Art for its exhibition "Twenty Centuries of Mexican Art" in 1940.

111

Ben Shahn. American, born Lithuania. 1898–1969. To U.S.A. 1906. *Willis Avenue Bridge.* 1940. Tempera on paper over composition board, 23 x 31⅜ inches. Gift of Lincoln Kirstein. [227.47]

The presence of the Mexican muralists in the United States during the 'twenties and 'thirties (see pages 110 and 111) had an important influence on artistic developments in this country. Their work set a precedent in technique, style, and content for many American artists who, in rebellion against the domination of foreign—especially French—art, were seeking to develop a native school of painting based on regional themes, and whose attention was focused on social problems as a major subject for art by the Great Depression that began in 1929. In 1933 the government, embarking for the first time in our history on wide-scale art patronage, initiated programs to give work to unemployed artists. Some created murals for public buildings, others produced easel paintings, and photographers were recruited to record the devastating effects that the Depression and prolonged years of drought had upon the farm population.

Ben Shahn was among those engaged in the photographic project. Previously, he had been hired by Diego Rivera to work as an assistant on frescoes for Rockefeller Center. The *Willis Avenue Bridge,* however, was painted in 1940 as an independent work, though a few years later Shahn repeated the subject in murals for the Social Security Building in Washington. Using his own photographs as a basis, he freely synthesized elements from two of them for this picture. He declared: "Photographs give those details of form you think you'll remember but don't—details that I like to put in my paintings."

The symmetrical composition is dominated by the bright red struts of the bridge against the dark blue, cloudy sky. Their diagonals are crossed by the horizontal slats of the bench on which two elderly women sit side by side, rapt in separate concerns and gazing in opposite directions. Though this painting is of a type often classed as "social realism," Shahn has made no overt comment here but has contented himself with the role of objective reporter; nor can the *Willis Avenue Bridge* accurately be called realistic. All unnecessary details are eliminated from the composition, and Shahn has indulged in such distortions as truncating the legs of the bench and displacing them with relation to the elements of the bridge, and elongating the crutches to give them greater importance in both the design and the content of his picture.

JACOB LAWRENCE. American, born 1917. *The Migration of the Negro:* No. 48, "Housing for the Negroes was a very difficult problem"; No. 58, "In the North the Negro had better educational facilities." 1940–1941. Tempera on gesso ground on composition board, 18 x 12 inches and 12 x 18 inches. Gift of Mrs. David M. Levy. [28.42.24 and 29]

These are two of sixty paintings constituting *The Migration of the Negro* (the thirty with odd numbers being owned by the Phillips Collection in Washington and the thirty with even numbers by The Museum of Modern Art). The pictures and their accompanying captions tell how, beginning about 1916, thousands of blacks left the poverty, discrimination, and brutality they found in the South to seek work opportunities in the more industrialized North. Lawrence has pointed out, "My parents were a part of this migration—on their way North when I was born in Atlantic City in 1917." The family moved to Harlem when he was a youngster, and the paintings in the series reflect his personal experiences, which he supplemented by extensive research on the migration.

Lawrence began painting as a child, and the tempera medium he uses is a natural outgrowth of the poster paints given him then. His pure colors and the flat, simplified compositions of his pictures also suggest posters. After attending a number of art schools, he was employed in 1938 on the easel division of the Federal Art Project; thereafter, a fellowship enabled him to continue research and develop *The Migration of the Negro*.

Among the artists whom he has admired, Lawrence has placed Orozco (page 111) in first rank, followed by Daumier and Goya, because "they're forceful. Simple. Human." These adjectives well apply to Lawrence's own work. He relies on clear, forthright statements rather than on rhetoric, and on the cumulative effect of the individual episodes within the narrative. As regards his style, he has said: "My work is abstract in the sense of having been designed and composed, but it is not abstract in the sense of having no human content. In your work, the human subject is the most important thing. An abstract style is simply your way of speaking. As far as you yourself are concerned, you want to communicate. I want the idea to strike right away."

ANDRÉ DERAIN. French, 1880-1954. *London Bridge.* 1906. Oil on canvas, 26 x 39 inches. Gift of Mr. and Mrs. Charles Zadok. [195.52]

Even the most ardent admirers of London are not apt to think of it in terms of vivid color; but in the *London Bridge,* Derain transmuted the city's grayness into brilliant blues, greens, reds, yellows, and oranges, accented with black. The vehement brushstrokes recall those of van Gogh (page 16), one of the major early influences on Derain's art; but the bright, unnaturalistic color probably owes more to Matisse, who befriended and encouraged the younger artist and was responsible for persuading his parents to allow him to become a full-time painter.

In the summer of 1905, Derain joined Matisse in Collioure on the southwest coast of France; and he was among the group whose paintings, shown at the Salon d'Automne in the fall of that year, profoundly shocked the critics by their "formless confusion of colors, blue, red, yellow, green, splotches of pigment crudely juxtaposed; the barbaric and naïve sport of a child who plays with a box of colors he has just got as a Christmas present." Matisse and his circle of artists were shortly dubbed *Fauves* ("wild beasts"). Some years later, Derain

wrote: "Fauvism was our ordeal by fire.... Colors became charges of dynamite. They were expected to discharge light.... The great merit of this method was to free the picture from all imitative and conventional contact." Unlike many of the Fauves, however, Derain was determined to paint in terms of volumetric form as well as in decorative patterns of color, and he resisted the prevailing trend toward flatness, as the composition of the *London Bridge* clearly shows. The stone piers are anchored solidly amid the swirling waters, and an entirely traditional perspective leads the eye back to the buildings on the farther shore.

Derain visited London in 1905 and again in 1906. This picture belongs to a series of London views that he was commissioned to make by his dealer, Ambroise Vollard, who wished them to be a kind of sequel to Monet's views of the Thames that had been shown at his gallery with great success in 1904. Writing to his friend Vlaminck, another Fauve, Derain said that though he believed Monet "had been right to render with his fugitive and fleeting color the natural impression which is no more than an impression . . . I am looking for something different—something which, on the contrary, is fixed, eternal, and complex."

LYONEL FEININGER. American, 1871–1956. In Germany 1887–1936; returned to U.S.A. 1937. *Viaduct.* 1920. Oil on canvas, 39¾ x 33¾ inches. Acquired through the Lillie P. Bliss Bequest. [259.44]

Feininger's *Viaduct* presents a soaring, clearly delineated structure, bathed in radiant light. Both its mood of timeless serenity and its technique contrast sharply with Derain's *London Bridge*, which shows a major artery of communication with teeming traffic passing over it and boats busily plying the waters below, painted with energetic brushstrokes that convey the turbulence of a modern metropolis.

At the age of sixteen, Feininger left his native America and went to live in Germany, where he remained for fifty years. He came in contact with Cubism in 1911 when he exhibited some of his paintings at the Salon des Indépendants in Paris. At the same time, he became acquainted with Delaunay (page 33), whose preoccupation with color and the way in which light modifies observed reality paralleled Feininger's own interests. Unlike the French Cubists, Feininger wanted his paintings to express "the principle of monumentality"; their broken planes of color and light were never used to break up forms but rather to give them a crystalline clarity. Many of his pictures are of architectural subjects, and in these works, as Hans Hess has noted: "The emotional content . . . is often romantic. The form found for the content is classical in order and law."

In a letter written to his friend Alfred Kubin in 1913, Feininger said: "I could not choose the purely abstract form, because then all progress ceases. . . . One has only to refine one's eyes, study *intensively* problems of light, problems of the volume of light and color; and then one sees that the laws of nature are as strict as any mathematical law that man can formulate."

Feininger painted the *Viaduct* at the Bauhaus in Weimar before its removal to Dessau. He had been summoned as teacher when the school was founded in 1919 and was soon joined by such other artists as Schlemmer (page 67) and Klee (page 99). Like the *Viaduct*, the pictures Feininger produced during his Bauhaus period are characterized by large, luminous planes. The forms themselves seem to generate light, and the thin oil medium has almost the transparency of watercolor.

HENRI MATISSE. French, 1869-1954. *The Moroccans.* 1915-1916. Oil on canvas, 71⅜ inches x 9 feet 2 inches. Gift of Mr. and Mrs. Samuel A. Marx. [386.55]

Unlike Derain's *London Bridge* (page 114), *The Moroccans* does not represent a specific scene recently viewed but is a synthesis of Matisse's impressions of Tangier, where he had spent the winters of 1912 and 1913. As described by Alfred H. Barr, Jr.: "The picture is divided into three sections, separate both as regards composition and subject matter: at the upper left one sees a terrace or balcony with a pot of large blue flowers at the corner, a small mosque beyond and, above, the lattice of a pergola; below, on a pavement, is a pile of four yellow melons with their great green leaves; and at the right are half a dozen Moroccans, one of them seated in the foreground with his back turned; the others, extremely abstract in design, are reclining or crouching with burnouses drawn over their heads. These three groups might be described as compositions of architecture, still life and figures. They are like three movements within a symphony—with well-marked intermissions—or perhaps three choirs of instruments within the orchestra itself.

"The three major groupings of *The Moroccans* are . . . ordered around an empty center and against a background which is two-thirds black with a left-hand third in color—though as Matisse remarked . . . he was using black as a 'color of light' not darkness. The black in *The Moroccans* in fact does seem as brilliant as the lavender. . . . Linear perspective is almost eliminated, the artist having silhouetted the objects in tiers as in an Egyptian relief. He does however diminish the more remote forms, thereby implying distance without sacrificing the clarity and immediacy of the images. . . .

"The analogies and ambiguities which enrich the composition of *The Moroccans* are ingenious. The four great round flowers in the architecture section echo the four melons in the still-life section. Yet these melons are so like the turban of the seated Moroccan in the figure section that the whole pile of melons with their leaves has sometimes been interpreted as Moroccans bowing their foreheads to the ground in prayer. At the same time, to complete the circle, some of the figures are so abstractly constructed as to suggest analogies with the architecture section. Thus Matisse, in one of his greatest paintings, sets up a polyphony of both formal and representational analogues."

116

MILTON AVERY. American, 1893–1965. *Sea Grasses and Blue Sea.* 1958. Oil on canvas, 60⅛ inches x 6 feet ⅜ inch. Gift of friends of the artist. [649.59]

Though the *Sea Grasses and Blue Sea* is based on nature, its elements have been so stringently reduced that it seems almost abstract. Avery has distilled his recollections of Provincetown into the simplest of compositional schemes, held together by subtle color harmonies. Beneath the narrow horizontal band of sky at the top, the remainder of the canvas is divided diagonally into two trapezoids of almost equal area. The sea grasses below present a surface that is lightly streaked, and of the same tonality as the sky, but paler. By contrast, the water above ranges from a very light blue to a deeply saturated hue, broken by the waves, which are painted black, rimmed and flecked with white foam. The black here does indeed seem, as in Matisse's *Moroccans,* to be a "color of light" rather than of darkness.

Avery has, in fact, often been compared to Matisse, though his development took place entirely in America, and he did not make his first trip to Europe until 1952, when he was nearly sixty. Any similarity between the two artists is attributable less to a direct influence than to a like attitude toward painting. Avery appears to have shared Matisse's view that a picture must be a "condensation of sensations," achieved through composition—"the art of arranging in a decorative manner the various elements at the painter's disposal for the expression of his feelings." He also believed that, as Matisse declared, "the chief aim of color should be to serve expression as well as possible," and that the choice of color, though based on observation, should depend on "instinct and sensibility."

A highly original artist, Avery followed his own bent, developing a lyrical mode almost totally independent of the prevailing styles in American art during most of his lifetime. The chromatic sensibility of his late paintings, such as the *Sea Grasses and Blue Sea,* has won increasing respect among more recent color abstractionists. The critic Clement Greenberg wrote: "His art demonstrates how sheer truth of feeling can galvanize what seem the most inertly decorative elements—a tenuous flatness; pure, largely valueless contrasts of hue; large, unbroken tracts of uniform color; an utter, unaccented simplicity of design—into tight and dramatic unities."

JOSEPH PICKETT. American, 1848–1918. *Manchester Valley.* 1914–1918? Oil with sand on canvas, $45\frac{1}{2}$ x $60\frac{5}{8}$ inches. Gift of Abby Aldrich Rockefeller. [541.39]

Pickett was a canal-boat builder, carpenter, and in his later years a storekeeper of New Hope, Pennsylvania, who took up painting toward the end of his life. The large building that dominates this view of his native town is the schoolhouse, in which the painting hung for many years as a gift from Pickett's widow, who had bought it for a dollar when it was put up for auction after his death.

The strong sense for decorative patterning that distinguishes many of the best works by self-taught artists is especially evident in the *Manchester Valley.* In order to show every detail clearly, Pickett made no attempt at scientific perspective but tilted the scene upward and arranged his objects in tiers one above the other, as in ancient Egyptian reliefs or Oriental landscapes. The trees in the distance are as large as those in the foreground, and the sides of the buildings shown as completely as their façades. The delicate foliage of the trees does not mask the lacy network of their branches; the rhythmic verticals and horizontals of fence posts and rails are matched by the lines of the railroad tracks and ties; the flow of the river current is repeated in the puff of steam issuing from the engine and the clouds streaming across the sky. Each brick or square of masonry is distinct, and the repeated rectangles of the windowpanes are as bright as if they were illuminated from within, though this is a daytime scene. The oversize flag on the schoolhouse shows off the stars and stripes to full advantage, and the train is painted with the gay colors of a child's toy.

A meticulous craftsman, Pickett made his own brushes and invented his own technique. In the *Manchester Valley,* he mixed his paint with sand, building up his forms in low relief and giving each surface a special texture.

CHARLES SHEELER. American, 1883-1965. *American Landscape.* 1930. Oil on canvas, 24 x 31 inches. Gift of Abby Aldrich Rockefeller. [166.34]

The elements of this landscape are essentially the same as those in Pickett's *Manchester Valley*: a river in the foreground flanked by a railroad track and train, with buildings beyond. At first sight, by comparison with Pickett's painting, the view seems to have been rendered with photographic realism. Sheeler was, in fact, a master of the camera, besides being a painter, and the *American Landscape* was based on one of a series of photographs of the Ford plant at River Rouge, Michigan, which he had been commissioned to make in 1927. When we look more closely, however, we realize that no camera could have captured the scene with such allover exactitude, without the slightest atmospheric blurring of the sharp outlines and clean surfaces. Every accidental detail has been eliminated; no factory and railroad siding could possibly be so free from any trace of grime.

Early in his career, Sheeler had been influenced by Cubism. Attracted by the mechanical themes of our in-dustrial civilization, he was one of a group of artists who, in the 'twenties, attempted a compromise between the principles of abstract art and the realistic representation of modern America. Because of the smooth, precise technique adopted by these artists, who used flat, even areas of color to emphasize the geometrical simplicity of the forms in their paintings, they were known as the Immaculates or Precisionists.

The *American Landscape,* like all pictures by Sheeler, has a firm compositional structure. A strong pattern of verticals is established by the curved walls of the buildings at the left, the high smokestack, the chute at the right, and their reflections in the calm water. As counterpoint to these vertical accents is a sequence of repeated parallel lines of varying lengths running across the face of the canvas at slightly different angles. There is a skillful, rhythmic alternation of lights and darks. The longer we look at this landscape, the more we perceive that its seeming realism has been achieved through carefully calculated artifice—"the painting being," in Sheeler's words, "the result of a composite image and the photograph being the result of a single image."

ANDREW WYETH. American, born 1917. *Christina's World.* 1948. Tempera on gesso panel, 32¼ x 47¾ inches. Purchase. [16.49]

This is the best known of several paintings of Christina Olson, who with her brother, a former fisherman turned truck gardener, was a neighbor of Wyeth's in Maine. Christina, severely crippled by polio, possessed a keen mind and a love of nature. Wyeth said: "The challenge to me was to do justice to her extraordinary conquest of a life which most people would consider hopeless. Christina's world is outwardly limited—but in this painting I tried to convey how unlimited it really is."

The direct inspiration for the picture was a glimpse of Christina that Wyeth caught one day when she was out picking berries and stopped to gaze back across the field toward her house. As in all his best paintings, there are few elements in the composition, and what seems to be a very simple subject, realistically depicted, has evocative implications. Taking as his point of departure a momentary impression, Wyeth has recorded it by a slow and painstaking procedure, in an effort to capture the minutiae of texture and the effects of light and shade. The tempera medium that he uses is an exacting one, well suited to his precise draughtsmanship and methodical manner of constructing his paintings through the accumulation of small, delicate strokes.

The separate blades of grass and the strands of Christina's hair are rendered with greater distinctness than the eye would register them, and the cast shadows, such as those of Christina's right arm and the ladder leaning against the wall of the house, are seen in sharp focus. This type of painting has been called "magic realism," because it invests ordinary objects with poetic mystery. Though seemingly very different from de Chirico's "metaphysical" painting, Wyeth's *Christina's World,* like *The Nostalgia of the Infinite* (page 85), exploits the romantic suggestions that are implicit in deep perspective and the use of a high horizon line, against which buildings are silhouetted.

EDWARD HOPPER. American, 1882–1967. *Gas*. 1940. Oil on canvas, 26¼ x 40¼ inches. Mrs. Simon Guggenheim Fund. [577.43]

Like most of his pictures, Hopper's *Gas* shows a commonplace of the American scene, painted in a way that both sharpens our perception of it and makes us feel an underlying sense of mystery. The ostensible subject here is an ordinary gas station manned by a lone attendant; the real subject, however, is light and atmosphere. Daylight has not quite faded from the darkening sky, allowing us still to see some colors of the landscape; but the electric lights have already been turned on, and their rays stream from the doors and windows of the building, the tops of the pumps, and the lamp on the signboard. The play of conflicting kinds of illumination of varying intensity, coming from different sources, changes the colors of the trees, grass, and plants bordering the road, and there is a contrast between the sharp-edged reflections at the right of the picture and the atmospheric blurring on the opposite side.

The composition has been designed with an almost geometrical structure. The receding diagonals of the trees, highway, base of the pumps, and buildings are intersected by a succession of verticals—the walls, windows, door, and turret of the house, the upright signpost, the pumps, and the figure of the man. For all its apparent realism, Hopper's *Gas* is a composite, in which he combined details studied from nature with parts observed from several sources, to create the image he had in mind.

Hopper once said: "My aim in painting has always been the most exact transcription possible of my most intimate impressions of nature." His picture *Gas* is imbued with strong subjective emotion. In this connection, Lloyd Goodrich wrote of Hopper's work: "This emotion was concentrated not on humanity but on its environment, on the structures and objects that man has built, and on nature with its signs of man's activities. A gasoline station on a country road with night coming on, its lighted red pumps bright against dark woods and cold evening sky—this familiar image expresses all the loneliness of the traveller at nightfall. . . . In exactly conveying the mood of . . . particular places and hours, Hopper's art transcended realism and became highly personal poetry. His poetry was never sentimental; it had too direct a relation to actualities."

CHAIM SOUTINE. French, born Lithuania. 1893–1943. To France 1913. *The Old Mill.* c. 1922–1923. Oil on canvas, 26⅛ x 32⅜ inches. Vladimir Horowitz and Bernard Davis Funds. [557.54]

Nothing in the actual scene represented in Soutine's landscape—an old mill set in the hilly countryside of Cagnes in Provence, surrounded by trees, with a road ascending at the right to a house in the background, and only a small segment of sky visible—would lead one to expect the violent deformations and turbulent rhythms apparent in this painting. Everything in the picture slants decisively to the right and is twisted as if by an earthquake or hurricane; in Monroe Wheeler's words, "the architecture becomes flexible and billows like a canvas, the trees reel and stumble about, and the colors seem to have been wrested hungrily from the spectrum."

In developing his own type of expressionism, Soutine was influenced by such old masters as Tintoretto, El Greco, and Rembrandt; by van Gogh, whose *Starry Night* (page 16) seems almost placid by comparison with *The Old Mill;* and by the bold color schemes of Bonnard (page 27). Soutine went further than any of these predecessors toward abstraction; but nature, no matter how transformed by emotion, was always his point of departure.

Soutine's style during this phase of his career has been regarded as anticipating in some respects that of the American Abstract Expressionists, which developed more than a quarter of a century later. In a perceptive article written in 1950, the artist Jack Tworkov pointed out analogies to Soutine's work in that of some of his own colleagues—notably Willem de Kooning, whose *Woman, I* (page 131) had not yet been painted, and Jackson Pollock (page 139). Tworkov referred especially to Soutine's "completely impulsive use of pigment as a material; . . . the absence of any effacing of the tracks bearing the imprint of the energy passing over the surface. . . . The artist's attitude toward the commonplace things that fill his picture . . . assumes that the relation between the subject (the painter) and the object is not fixed, but that the object, the more deeply it is experienced, changes, changing also the attitude of the painter towards the object. And it assumes that this process goes on continually throughout the duration of the creative act. . . . Hence the fluidity of the image, the unpredictability of its outline, the 'shake'; and in a flash it explains why Soutine's subjects, in spite of violent distortions, have such intense reality."

JOHN MARIN. American, 1870–1953. In Paris 1905–1910. *Lower Manhattan (Composing Derived from Top of Woolworth)*. 1922. Watercolor and charcoal with paper cutout attached with thread, 21⅝ x 26⅞ inches. Acquired through the Lillie P. Bliss Bequest. [143.45]

Like Soutine's *Old Mill*, Marin's *Lower Manhattan* is imbued with the artist's intense emotion before the scene he depicts. His vantage point was the top of the Woolworth Building, then the world's tallest skyscraper. "From this dizzy height," Alfred H. Barr, Jr. has written, "the eye plunges into the zigzag perspectives of buildings and car-dotted streets, grinding out to sea like a dynamited ice flow." Lines radiate outward from the rounded shape at the bottom with a yellow sunburst stitched to its center, inspired by the gilded dome of the now-demolished Pulitzer Building in Park Row. Above is the blue and white background of water and sky.

Returning to New York in 1910 after a five-year sojourn in Paris, Marin was captivated by the "beautiful, fantastic" spectacle of the city's soaring buildings and the dynamic tempo of its traffic. In the catalogue of his one-man exhibition in 1913, he defended the "non-photographic" character of the fourteen watercolors of New York it included, saying that: "The whole city is alive; the buildings, people, all are alive; and the more they move me the more I feel them to be alive. It is this 'moving of me' that I try to express. . . . I see great forces at work; great movements; the large buildings and the small buildings; the warring of the great and the small; influences of one mass on another greater or smaller mass. . . . While these powers are at work pushing, pulling, sideways, downwards, upwards, I can hear the sound of their strife and there is great music being played."

The watercolor *Lower Manhattan* was painted almost a decade later, after Marin had developed a style even further removed from exact representation. Taking up again the theme of the city, he charged his paintings of New York with an explosive energy, expressed through plunging diagonals, bold outlines, and brilliant color. The fragmented planes and the irregular frame-within-a-frame surrounding the buildings are devices derived from Cubism, which Marin used in a highly personal manner to reconcile the illusionistic space of the view with the flatness he desired in his picture. The compositional scheme with paths of energy radiating outward from a circular nucleus also owes something to Futurist works by such artists as Boccioni (page 55).

ERNST LUDWIG KIRCHNER. German, 1880–1938. *Street, Dresden.* 1908 (dated on painting 1907). Oil on canvas, 59¼ x 6 feet 6⅞ inches. Purchase. [12.51]

The attitude of modern artists toward the city has varied according to their individual temperaments, some finding it exhilarating, as did Marin (page 123), others alienating, decadent, and conducive to anxiety. The avenue shown in Kirchner's *Street, Dresden* is thronged with figures who, in spite of their physical proximity, seem almost oblivious of one another. Their faces are masks assumed to hide their private selves from the public gaze. This effect of masquerade is accentuated by their unnatural coloring, which is keyed to the strident tonality of the whole composition.

Late in life, Kirchner said, "My goal was always to express emotion and experience with large and simple forms and clear colors." Earlier, he stated that his aim was "to give pictorial form to contemporary life." He was the dominant personality among several young artists in Dresden who banded together in 1905 to form the first group of German Expressionists. They called themselves *Die Brücke* ("The Bridge"), because they wished to constitute a bridge between traditional art and modern modes that were still being formulated. The establishment of Die Brücke coincides with that of the looser association of the Fauves in France (see page 114); both groups, reacting against Impressionism, exploited bold distortion and unnatural color.

In common with many avant-garde artists in the early years of the twentieth century who did not wish to abandon representation but, rather, adapt it in accordance with new pictorial concepts, Kirchner faced the problem of maintaining an illusion of depth in his canvas, while at the same time asserting its essential flatness. In the *Street, Dresden,* he has skillfully coordinated spatial recession with surface design—a design greatly enlivened by the women's flamboyant headgear. In the foreground, in the right half of the composition, life-size figures advance toward us in strict frontality. Their curving silhouettes stand out clearly in contrast to the pink road that leads the eye up and back toward the top of the picture. There, the tram in the center and a crowd of densely massed pedestrians completely shut off any opening toward a more distant space, resulting in a claustrophobic sense of constriction and tension.

JEAN DUBUFFET. French, born 1901. *Business Prospers.* 1961. Oil on canvas, 65 inches x 7 feet 2⅝ inches. Mrs. Simon Guggenheim Fund. [115.62]

In the *Business Prospers,* as in the *Street, Dresden,* city-dwellers are shown as crowded together yet psychologically apart. To signify their isolation from their fellows, Dubuffet has enclosed them in cells, within which they carry on their separate activities. Unlike Kirchner, Dubuffet makes no attempt to portray realistic figures in three-dimensional space. Instead, he has filled his entire canvas with a jumbled panorama of buildings, personages, and vehicles—some upright, some sideways, some upside down. They and the graffitilike inscriptions are all drawn in a deliberately childlike fashion, in keeping with Dubuffet's admiration for the creative expression of children, self-taught artists, and the insane (see page 130). There is nothing naïve, however, in his attitude toward the city and its inhabitants, as is evident from the painting's satirical title and the legends parodying signs on shop fronts and public buildings. They testify to his opinion that Paris is peopled by rascals and scoundrels of every description, characterized by greed and hypocrisy. At the upper center, for example, the fascia of the "Gro-

tesque Bank" appears above the words "At the Funereal Smile"; the establishments next door are identified as "At the Sign of the Thief" and "The Short-Weight Shop." Below the blue oblong of the Chancellery at the center right is the "Ministry of Greasy Paws."

This picture is one of a series called Paris Circus, which preoccupied Dubuffet in 1961–1962. During the previous seven years, he had been living in Vence in the south of France, devoting himself almost exclusively to themes drawn from nature and the countryside. Returning to Paris for his first extended sojourn since 1955, he took up again with enthusiasm the subject of the city, which had engaged him some twenty years before.

Beyond Dubuffet's caustic humor is another intent: to impart a magical sense of wonder to everyday persons, objects, and occurrences. "Every work of art should in the highest degree lift one out of context, provoking a surprise and a shock," he declared. Of his Paris Circus, he wrote: "What I wish is to give a phantasmagoric character to the locale evoked by the painting, and this can be done only by mingling elements that are more or less true to life with interposed features that are arbitrary and unreal. I want my street to be mad, and to have my sidewalks, shops, and buildings participate in a crazy dance."

125

STUART DAVIS. American, 1894–1964. *Visa.* 1951. Oil on canvas, 40 x 52 inches. Gift of Mrs. Gertrud A. Mellon. [9.53]

Whereas in his *Business Prospers* (page 125) Dubuffet recognized the important role that signs play in the modern cityscape, Davis went even further in his *Visa* and made words the dominant subject matter of his painting. "We see words everywhere in modern life; we're bombarded by them," he said. "But physically words are also shapes. You don't want banal boring words any more than you want banal boring shapes or a banal boring life."

Davis's selection of words is somewhat arbitrary, based in part on their shapes and in part on their associations. This composition is one of several having as their central feature the word "Champion," which was suggested by nothing more significant than the name of a brand of spark plugs printed on a book of matches. The final form of the letters, their color, and their arrangement, however, have no connection whatever with that source. Davis explained that he chose "else" because it answered his need for a short word that would have no specific associative meaning to divert the spectator's attention; it "nevertheless has a fundamental dynamic content which consists of the thought of something else being possible and is therefore in harmony with the dynamic color intervals of the painting as a whole." The phrase "the amazing continuity," besides being necessary for "animating the area at the extreme right," refers to his experience of seeing in paintings of completely different subject matter and style a mysterious common factor—the "amazing continuity" that unites them as works of art. "Therefore the content of this phrase is real," Davis said, "as real as any shape of a face or a tree." His signature also is an integral part of the design, not an extraneous adjunct. As for the title *Visa,* he called it "a secret. Because I believe in magic."

Davis declared that all his pictures (including those painted in Paris in 1928–1929) "have their originating impulse in the impact of the contemporary American environment"—the tempo of New York City, its ubiquitous signboards, its cacophony, and the basic rhythms of jazz. Bright colors used in combination with black are his essential means for defining space relationships and determining the "events" that take place within his compositions. In the *Visa,* as in most of his paintings, color is applied in flat areas, with no textural effects that might detract from the firm clarity of the design elements.

JAMES ROSENQUIST. American, born 1933. *Marilyn Monroe, I*. 1962. Oil and spray enamel on canvas, 7 feet 9 inches x 6 feet ¼ inch. The Sidney and Harriet Janis Collection. [646.67]

Even more specifically than Davis's *Visa,* the *Marilyn Monroe, I* reflects the visual impact of outdoor advertising signs. Rosenquist, in fact, earned his living for several years as a sign painter, perched high on scaffolds above Broadway and other sites in New York while he worked on enormous billboards. Though he had attended art schools, Rosenquist has said that it was actually from his commercial experience that he learned the properties of paint, much as the self-taught artist John Kane profited by his painting of railroad cars (see page 64). The billboards also affected Rosenquist's sense of scale. He discovered that if an image, such as the fragment of a face or an object, is painted in gigantic size, it becomes as immediately unrecognizable as if it were brought up directly under the viewer's nose. In the process of losing its identity, it becomes primarily form.

Around 1960, Rosenquist was one of the first of a number of young artists to come to terms with modern urban life and America's industrialized landscape by incorporating their most vulgar banalities into art. The public and the majority of critics at the time tended to see this chiefly as a reaction to Abstract Expressionism and a return to representation. In their concentration on the themes portrayed, they failed to perceive the formal qualities inherent in the work of the so-called Pop artists. Rosenquist, however, has stated firmly that the objects he paints do not, as such, constitute his subject: "The relationships between them may be the subject matter, the relationships of the fragments I do. The content will be something more . . . will, hopefully, be fatter, balloon to more than the subject matter. One thing, though, the subject matter isn't popular images, it isn't that at all."

This portrait of the ill-fated film star was painted shortly after her death. Her face, fragmented and divided among compartments as if it were a collage, appears upside down behind the huge silvery letters of her name, partially spelled out, as is the word "Coca-Cola" that drifts across like skywriting. By this juxtaposition, Rosenquist has subtly implied that her fame had entrenched Marilyn Monroe in American iconography as firmly as the soft drink, thus making her equally an expendable consumer product. He recalls having painted the picture in an exceptionally short time, "as short as her career and her life."

127

ROY LICHTENSTEIN. American, born 1923. *Drowning Girl.* 1963. Oil and synthetic polymer paint on canvas, 67⅝ x 66¾ inches. Philip Johnson Fund and Gift of Mr. and Mrs. Bagley Wright. [685.71]

The imagery and techniques of commercial art are an even more obvious point of departure for the *Drowning Girl* than for Rosenquist's *Marilyn Monroe, I* (page 127). When in the early 'sixties Lichtenstein first exhibited paintings such as this, based on comic strips, the shock to accepted ideas of what constitutes "art" and the contrast with the still-prevailing style of Abstract Expressionism were so great that the formal qualities of his works were almost entirely overlooked.

With ironic humor, Lichtenstein selects images that are both stereotyped and ubiquitous in our culture. His models are neither living, three-dimensional figures nor photographs, but flat representations already far removed from naturalism by the artificial conventions of cartooning. Highly decorative and abstract, cartoon style has in large part been determined by the requirements of cheap commercial printing. It is characterized by a few primary colors, applied either in flat areas or with benday dots for shading and tinting, and by drawing with broad outlines to mask the overlapping of colors that may occur when many thousands of copies on newsprint are rolled off the presses. In this picture, the blue of the girl's hair—the same color as that used for the dots in the waves—still further removes from the subject any sense of reality.

By isolating one frame from a comic strip's serial mode of narration and enlarging the figure to over life size, Lichtenstein has greatly altered the impact that his image has upon the viewer, by comparison with its model. Furthermore, he has not slavishly copied that prototype. He has altered it by such devices as cropping, manipulated its forms into a unified, allover pattern, and exaggerated certain features of its style. Lichtenstein has pointed out that, intentionally or not, cartooning already resembles other kinds of art, and he makes these similarities more explicit and recognizable: "In the *Drowning Girl,* the water is not only Art Nouveau, but it can be seen as Hokusai. . . . I saw it and then pushed it a little further until it was a reference that most people will get." Another such reference is the suggestion of Seurat's pointillist technique (see page 17) implicit in the simulated benday dots. These can be read in two ways, as Lichtenstein has noted: "Dots can mean printed surface and therefore 'plane' but in contradiction, particularly in large areas, they become atmospheric and intangible—like sky."

The balloon caption is incorporated as a functioning element of the total design. There is an inherent paradox in the incongruity between the urgent emotional content of its message and the picture's wholly depersonalized style and technique; but the emotion conveyed is in itself as trite and synthetic as that in comic strips and soap operas.

FERNAND LÉGER. French, 1881–1955. In U.S.A. 1940–1945. *Big Julie.* 1945. Oil on canvas, 44 x 50⅛ inches. Acquired through the Lillie P. Bliss Bequest. [141.45]

A generation before young American artists like Rosenquist began to use Pop culture as a basis for their work, the French master Léger discovered that "bad taste is one of the valuable raw materials" of this country. As an artist in exile during the Occupation of France, Léger lived in the United States from 1940 to 1945 and traveled extensively across the continent. He was impressed by America's "vitality, its litter and its waste," its quest for novelty, its dynamism, and "the contrast between the mechanical and the natural." Especially, he pointed out: "Bad taste—strong colors—it is all here for the painter to organize and get the full use of its power. Girls in sweaters with brilliant colored skin; girls in shorts dressed more like acrobats in a circus than one would ever come across on a Paris street. If I had only seen girls dressed in 'good taste' here I would never have painted my Cyclist series, of which *Big Julie* in The Museum of Modern Art was the culmination."

Needless to say, Léger transformed this raw material in accordance with his own predilections and distinctive style. The *Big Julie* combines his love for machine forms and for the stylized human figure, manifest in such earlier works as the *Exit the Ballets Russes* (page 66) and the *Three Women* (page 71). Despite the extreme simplification of drawing and modeling, and the use of gray and black instead of natural flesh tones, the cyclist is a far more supple and feminine creature than the stolid women at breakfast in the latter canvas. Léger's fondness for clearly defined patterns is evident throughout the *Big Julie,* in combination with strong colors chosen to show off the shapes of the figures and objects to full advantage. The black background at the left contrasts sharply with the cyclist's gray body, red hat with spiky cockade, and orange suit, against which is silhouetted a big yellow flower with green leaves. At the right, a dark red cross is superimposed on a yellow background. The color and angularity of these shapes serve as foil for the woman's rounded arm and the rhythmic, interlacing curves of her bicycle. The two blue butterflies are gay accents punctuating the black and yellow fields.

129

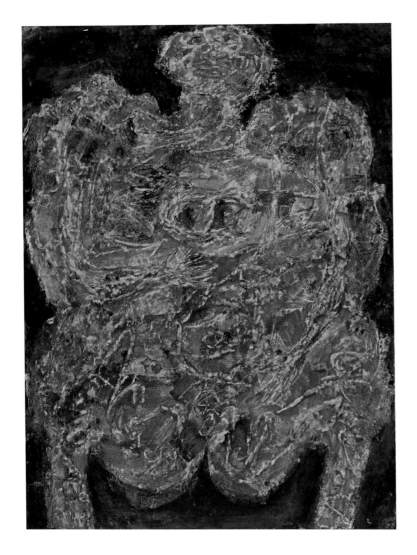

JEAN DUBUFFET. French, born 1901. *Corps de Dame: Blue Short Circuit.* 1951. Oil on canvas, 46⅛ x 35¼ inches. The Sidney and Harriet Janis Collection. [593.67]

From the standpoint of female pulchritude, the naked women in Dubuffet's Corps de Dames series are even more shockingly repellent than those in Picasso's *Demoiselles d'Avignon* (page 47). But Dubuffet has explained that he had other criteria in mind when painting this theme: "The female body, of all objects in the world, is the one that has long been associated (for Occidentals) with a very specious notion of beauty (inherited from the Greeks and cultivated by the magazine covers); now it pleases me to protest against this aesthetic, which I find miserable and most depressing. . . . The beauty of an object depends on how we look at it and not at all on its proper proportions. . . . Certain people believe the mood of my art to be bitter. These people have seen that I intend to sweep away everything we have been taught to consider—without question—as grace and beauty, but have overlooked my effort to substitute another and vaster beauty. . . . I would like people to look at my work as an enterprise for the rehabilitation of scorned values and, in any case, make no mistake, a work of ardent celebration."

In a romantic quest for the wellsprings of "true art," Dubuffet repudiated classical canons in favor of "barbaric" art and rejected controlled and rational means of expression for art that was automatic, spontaneous, and even psychotic. Believing that creative impulses operate independently of cultural conventions, he has collected, exhibited, and extolled what he calls *l'art brut*—the raw expressions of primitives and the insane. Besides his "anticultural position," Dubuffet's other major preoccupation has been a passionate concern with materials and their properties. Abandoning traditional mediums and techniques, he endlessly develops new substances or "pastes" and works his surfaces with his fingers, incises them with sticks, or incorporates into them heterogeneous stuff.

In the *Corps de Dame: Blue Short Circuit,* the figure is cut off below the knees and crowded within the dimensions of the canvas. The head is small and flat, the body bloated. The tiny breasts are rendered in relief and encircled in blue, as is the navel; the exposed pubic area is emphasized as in paleolithic sculptures of the Earth Mother or fertility goddesses. If we are to find in this picture the beauty that Dubuffet would have us see, we must not judge the image as we would judge a living woman, but rather take pleasure in his vigorous rendering, with its swirling contours and exuberant handling of materials. As the title implies, the work is informed with an electric tension. The medium is generally fluid but in certain areas is worked into a thick impasto, with incised lines. The high-keyed, rosy color is intended to evoke the body's vital fluids.

WILLEM DE KOONING. American, born the Netherlands 1904. To U.S.A. 1926. *Woman, I.* 1950–1952. Oil on canvas, 6 feet 3⅞ inches x 58 inches. Purchase. [478.53]

At the very time that Dubuffet was involved with his *Corps de Dames*, de Kooning, a leading member of the Abstract Expressionist group in New York, was struggling to create this, the first of his Woman series. Besides producing quantities of preparatory drawings and studies, de Kooning was continually painting and repainting the canvas in what Harold Rosenberg has called a "synthesis of will and chance," allowing accidental effects to coexist with those deliberately planned. He worked on the picture for over two years before considering it completed, and at the last moment added a strip to the right side of the canvas so that the figure would be off center.

If Dubuffet's *Corps de Dame: Blue Short Circuit* is a celebration of some primordial, timeless Earth Mother, de Kooning's *Woman, I* is a savage travesty of the aggressive modern female. Though de Kooning says he had in mind the long classical tradition of woman as "the idol, the Venus, the nude," he also incorporated into this image references to such contemporary idols as pinup girls and the banal stereotypes found in billboard and magazine advertisements. These references are apparent in the large, ogling eyes, overdeveloped breasts, and toothy grin of the *Woman, I* (in one study for the picture, de Kooning actually pasted onto the canvas a color reproduction of a mouth cut from a cigarette ad). The final figure certainly seems far more predatory than seductive; but if the *Woman, I* reveals de Kooning's hostility toward womankind, he is said to have been disappointed that, when it was first exhibited, nobody noticed its comic aspect.

Obviously, de Kooning was at least as much concerned with the paint medium itself, and his handling of it, as with the subject he portrayed. In this respect, his attitude toward creative expression is analogous to the approaches of both Dubuffet and Appel (page 65). In the *Woman, I,* the brushstrokes do not, for the most part, outline the form or model them in a conventional way. They seem to have an independent life of their own, animating the entire surface with overlapping passages of pure color, so that one fragment of the canvas—or one part of the body—seems almost interchangeable with any other. The painting is, in fact, replete with ambiguities, such as the handling of space and the purposefully unidentifiable environment in which the figure is seated. De Kooning also observed that the woman's form reminded him strongly of "a landscape—with arms like lanes and a body of hills and fields, all brought up close to the surface, like a panorama squeezed together."

Henri Matisse. French, 1869–1954. *Memory of Oceania.* 1952–1953. Gouache and crayon on cut-and-pasted paper on canvas, 9 feet 4 inches x 9 feet 4⁷/₈ inches. Mrs. Simon Guggenheim Fund. [224.68]

The *Memory of Oceania,* one of the most abstract compositions that Matisse ever created, is not a portrayal of a tropical paradise so much as an evocation of his pleasurable, sensuous recollections of a visit to Tahiti made twenty-three years earlier. In its grandeur and its balance between studied simplification and subtle intricacy, it recalls works done many years previously, such as the *Piano Lesson* (page 69) and *The Moroccans* (page 116).

This huge composition, over nine feet square, was completed by Matisse at the age of eighty-four. In ill health, and confined to his bed or a wheelchair, he refused to allow infirmity to hamper his exuberant creativity. Unable to work at an easel, he developed on a monumental scale a medium with which he had first experimented in 1931. From sheets of paper painted with gouache in colors of his choosing, he cut out forms with a scissors and arranged them on a background. In the *Memory of Oceania,* he also used a black crayon to draw a few lines that magically conjure up the image of a reclining nude.

The orange border surrounding the picture is intercepted at intervals by bars of black. Within this frame, rectangles of differing proportions are combined with irregular shapes. The various forms in two shades of yellow, bright orange, its complementary blue, leaf green, magenta, and black are overlaid upon one another and set against the open white field with its crayon drawing. The prevailing impression of the composition, despite the flatness of all its elements, is one of airiness and space.

"There is no break between my painting and my cutouts," Matisse said. "Only, with something more of the abstract and the absolute, I have arrived at a distillation of form. . . . Of this or that object which I used to present in all its complexity in space, I now keep only the sign, which suffices . . . for the composition as I conceive it."

HANS HOFMANN. American, born Germany. 1880–1966. To U.S.A. 1932. *Memoria in Aeternum.* 1962. Oil on canvas, 7 feet x 6 feet ⅛ inch. Gift of the artist. [399.63]

The *Memoria in Aeternum,* like Matisse's *Memory of Oceania,* is a monumental painting produced when the artist was over eighty. Hofmann, however, still retained his vigorous health, and the works done in the last decade or so of his life are generally regarded as the crowning achievements of his long and active career. Though Hofmann was also, like Matisse, predominantly a colorist, in most respects their art differs markedly.

The rectangles in this painting—one bright yellow, the other bright red—do not overlap like those in the *Memory of Oceania* but are placed far apart. Instead of being set against open white space, they are given a background of murky brown streaked with red, yellow, and blue that covers almost the entire surface of the canvas. This ground brightens at the top, where an irregular trapezoid occupies the center of a truncated semicircular shape flanked with light blues. The openness at the upper corners repeats on a larger scale a small area of brightness at the lower left. Against the variegated brushwork of the background, the two rectangles seem to shift their positions vertically, as well as to recede and advance. Thus, a tension is set up between forms and space, between the flat plane of the canvas and the depth suggested by the implied movement of the shapes upon its surface. "The mystery of plastic creation is based upon the dualism of the two-dimensional and the three-dimensional," Hofmann declared; he called this dynamic interaction of flatness and depth "push and pull."

Throughout his life, Hofmann was both a theorist and an outstanding teacher. After coming to the United States, he first taught in California and subsequently opened schools in New York and Provincetown. Beginning about 1940, his work developed increasingly toward abstraction, and he was one of the principal formative influences on the "New American Painting" that began to emerge during that decade. Besides providing the stimulus of his own creative vitality, he was among the first in this country to encourage exploration of the possibilities of accidental effects in painting. He also advocated retention in the finished work of the clear traces of the painter's action in creating it—the paths of energy made by the gestures of his hand in its simultaneous response to his emotion and the properties inherent in the medium.

In the *Memoria in Aeternum,* Hofmann paid tribute to five dead American artists whom he had known and admired: his contemporary Arthur B. Carles, an early American Cubist, and four of the avant-garde abstractionists who came into prominence after the Second World War, who had all died while still in their prime—Arshile Gorky (page 41), Jackson Pollock (pages 83 and 139), Franz Kline (page 135), and Bradley Walker Tomlin (page 137).

133

CLYFFORD STILL. American, born 1904. *Painting.* 1951. Oil on canvas, 7 feet 10 inches x 6 feet 10 inches. Blanchette Rockefeller Fund. [277.54]

As in Hofmann's *Memoria in Aeternum* (page 133), almost the entire surface of this canvas is filled with a dark wall of paint, contrasting with a few areas of brightness. Still's *Painting,* however, contains no forms as clearly defined as the rectangles in Hofmann's picture to serve as focal points for the composition or mitigate the allover materiality of its dense surface. The heavy black impasto, enlivened with marks of the palette knife or brush, is intersected at the upper right and bordered at right and left with jagged streaks of brilliant color that seem to function as light. Though of very nearly the same proportions as the *Memoria in Aeternum,* Still's *Painting* produces a far greater effect of verticality. William Rubin has called such works by Still "Gothic," because their soaring, pointed forms are arranged in relation to one another and to the framing edges in a totally anticlassical way that calls to mind the structure of Gothic cathedrals.

On the other hand, Still himself has totally disavowed any associations between his paintings and either manmade objects or natural landscape. In a spirit that brings to mind Walt Whitman's boast, "I celebrate myself, and sing myself," he has said: "Each painting is an episode in a personal history, an entry in a journal. . . . I paint only myself, not nature." Repudiating all connection with any of the styles of modern art that evolved in Europe, he deliberately set himself the task of creating a completely new kind of painting, "cutting through all cultural opiates, past and present, so that a direct, immediate, and truly free vision could be achieved." He developed his highly original style on the West Coast, where he was an influential teacher. Even during his visits to New York and an eleven-year sojourn there from 1950 on, he held himself aloof from the other Abstract Expressionists. The monumental *Painting* of 1951 is characteristic of his pictures after his abandonment, in the mid-'forties, of all traces of imagery and illusionistic space.

FRANZ KLINE. American, 1910–1962. *Painting Number 2.* 1954. Oil on canvas, 6 feet 8½ inches x 8 feet 9 inches. Mr. and Mrs. Joseph H. Hazen and Mr. and Mrs. Francis F. Rosenbaum Funds. [236.69]

In contrast to the heavy dark wall of paint that looms up before us in Still's *Painting* is Kline's austere scaffolding of black bars intersecting open areas of white. For all its abstraction, his *Painting Number 2* invokes suggestions of modern machinery, or such urban structures as the steel girders of bridges or buildings in the process of erection.

The eye tends to read this configuration as drawn with bold black strokes on a white ground, in a manner resembling Oriental calligraphy enlarged to monumental scale; but closer inspection reveals that the white frequently cuts into and over the black. Kline pointed out that his work was in fact firmly based on Western tradition, "the tradition of painting the areas which, I think, came to its reality here through the work of Mondrian— in other words, everything was equally painted—I don't

mean that it's equalized, but I mean the white or the space is painted. . . ."

The impression of complete spontaneity that the picture gives is also somewhat misleading. Kline usually worked from preparatory sketches, although his actual execution was rapid, retaining the sense of gesture. He used the large brushes of house painters as well as the smaller ones generally employed by artists, and he favored commercial enamels, both because they were quick-drying and because they offered the possibility of contrasts between mat and glossy surfaces.

Except for some touches of bluish gray, this painting is rendered almost entirely in black and white, as were most of Kline's works from 1950 until shortly before his death. Following its rejection by the Impressionists, black as a "color" has been highly esteemed by many twentieth-century artists (see Matisse's comment, page 116). Among the Abstract Expressionists, both de Kooning and Pollock preceded Kline in creating many of their major paintings exclusively in black and white.

135

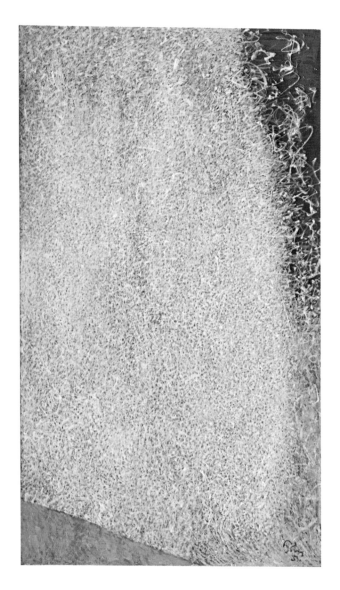

Mark Tobey. American, 1890–1976. To Switzerland 1960. *Edge of August*. 1953. Casein on composition board, 48 x 28 inches. Purchase. [5.54]

The *Edge of August* is not so much a representation of observed phenomena as an evocation of nature's processes. Tobey has said that in this picture he was "trying to express the thing that lies between two conditions of nature, summer and fall. It's trying to capture that transition and make it tangible. Make it sing." He explained that its more general significance was that "nature in her magnificent and mysterious ways creates changes through which we live and can gather wisdom for correspondences in our own lives.

This contemplative, mystical turn of mind is characteristic of Tobey. As a young man, he became a convert to the Baha'i World Faith, which teaches the indivisibility of ultimate reality, the oneness of all mankind, and progressive revelation leading to the eventual unification of all the peoples of the world. On visits to China and Japan, Tobey became familiar with Oriental art and thought, and during a sojourn in a Zen monastery tried unsuccessfully to master the practice of meditation.

Even before going to the Far East, however, he had begun to learn Chinese brushwork. This was to lead him to develop his distinctive calligraphic style, which in its dense intricacy nevertheless differs radically from the concise restraint of its Oriental sources. Calligraphy, which Kline's painting (page 135) only superficially resembles, is fundamental to Tobey's art. He has said that the theme of the *Edge of August* had been in his mind for about ten years before he painted it, but he was able to render it to his satisfaction only after having perfected what has been called his "white writing." "The painting is written," he said. "I built up the wall of fog in minute, rather structural strokes." The meshwork of tiny, pale lines seems to quiver and shift before one's eyes, revealing glimpses of iridescent color suggestive of space between and beyond the strokes. The field of calligraphy, bounded sharply at the lower left corner by a triangle of violet, dissipates gradually at the right side of the painting, which is filled with a ground that darkens almost to black at the top.

BRADLEY WALKER TOMLIN. American, 1899–1953. *Number 20*. 1949. Oil on canvas, 7 feet 2 inches x 6 feet 8¼ inches. Gift of Philip Johnson. [58.52]

In contrast to the intimacy of Tobey's *Edge of August* and its compact interweaving of minute brushstrokes, Tomlin's monumental, seven-foot-high canvas is filled with a bold calligraphy in which each character stands out clear and distinct. The light-toned bars and ribbons of angular, curving, and hooked signs, punctuated by small black and white squares and circles, seem like hieroglyphs that lack only the appropriate Rosetta Stone for their deciphering. They are deployed against a background of shifting rectangles, derived ultimately from the structural grid of such Cubist paintings as Picasso's *"Ma Jolie"*

(page 48). The sober color of Tomlin's *Number 20* of 1949, relieved only by a small red accent toward the top center, is also reminiscent of monochromatic Cubist paintings of 1911–1912.

The freely invented forms of his calligraphy, on the other hand, come out of a different tradition. They owe something to Surrealist automatism, one of the major formative influences on the avant-garde artists of the New York School, with whom Tomlin became associated in the late 'forties. His *Number 20,* however, cannot strictly be classified as "Abstract Expressionist," for besides its geometric underpinning, the signs, too, show a disciplined control rather than free spontaneity, and they are arranged in a formal design of austere, though decorative, elegance.

137

JACKSON POLLOCK. American, 1912–1956. *One (Number 31, 1950)*. 1950. Oil and enamel on canvas, 8 feet 10 inches x 17 feet 5⅝ inches. Gift of Sidney Janis. [7.68]

Pollock's immense, wall-size picture represents the apotheosis of calligraphic painting. Tobey's *Edge of August* (page 136) was "written" with delicate finger movements guiding the brush; the broader strokes in Tomlin's *Number 20* (page 137) evidence an ampler sweep of wrist and forearm; but the labyrinthine web of pigments in Pollock's *One* results from the action not of hand and arm alone, but of his entire body. In this as in his other "drip" paintings, enamel and oil paints were not only dripped but poured, spurted, or flung from sticks, brushes, or syringes as he walked around the canvas tacked to the floor. He said that he preferred working from all four sides in this way so that he could "literally *be* in the picture"; he likened the method to that of Indian sand painters of the West.

This technique enabled Pollock to unleash an exuberant—almost ecstatic—energy. Many critics and members of the public have been misled by his procedure into overestimating the degree of automatism involved in his painting. Pollock's automatism, however, was always held in check by his sense of rhythm, his intense concentration, and his virtuosity in controlling the direction, thickness, and continuity of the lines and drips. When accidental effects occurred, he incorporated them into the fabric of the whole by improvisation or, if they seemed aesthetically compatible, let them remain.

The title *One* refers to the concept of wholeness and unity expressed by the picture's allover patterning. By comparison with some of Pollock's more brightly colored paintings, this has a restrained palette of tans, blues, and grays, speckled and lashed through with black and white. The pigment is sometimes mat, sometimes glossy. In parts, its interwoven threads and clusters give texture to the surface; elsewhere, the paint is stained into the unprimed écru canvas. There is an effect of flickering light, with mysterious suggestions of depth lying beyond the surface.

The poet and critic Frank O'Hara has discussed the particular significance of scale in Pollock's large paintings and the emotional effect it has upon the spectator. Whereas artists of the past created a sense of scale in their murals through visual images that could be related either to the actual size of a man's body or to the building that the work would adorn, in Pollock's canvases there are no such points of reference. Thus, O'Hara writes: "The scale of the painting became that of the painter's body, not the image of a body, and the setting for the scale . . . the canvas surface itself. Upon this field the physical energies of the artist operate in actual detail, in full-scale . . . with no reference to exterior image or environment. It is scale, and no-scale. It is the physical reality of the artist and his activity of expressing it, united to the spiritual reality of the artist in a oneness which has no need for the mediation of metaphor or symbol."

HELEN FRANKENTHALER. American, born 1928. *Jacob's Ladder*. 1957. Oil on canvas, 9 feet 5⅜ inches x 69⅞ inches. Gift of Hyman N. Glickstein. [82.60]

When Pollock's *One* (page 139) and related paintings by him were first exhibited in 1951, they exerted a great influence on Helen Frankenthaler. Their scale, free graphic rhythms, and color impressed her strongly; but above all she was struck by Pollock's method of dripping paint directly onto the raw canvas, emphasizing both the flatness of the painting and the physical actuality of the support.

Carrying this technique still further, Frankenthaler thins her pigments with large amounts of turpentine so that they soak directly through the unprimed cloth and stain it. The resultant image no longer lies on top of the picture plane but is embedded within it; the transparent, mat colors of varying intensity modulate from light to dark without creating any illusion that they exist in a space other than that of the woven, textural surface. Frankenthaler also adopted Pollock's practice of painting with the canvas stretched out on the floor, allowing the artist to be "in" the picture, work from all four sides, and produce an image seen from above.

The rectangles and circles in the lower half of the *Jacob's Ladder* may be reminiscences of Frankenthaler's early training in the Cubist tradition, while the expressionist abandon of the upper section recalls her admiration for Kandinsky and Gorky (pages 40 and 41). These and other influences, however, are all assimilated within a style of notable originality.

Like many of her paintings, this picture contains within its abstract design certain allusive references. Such images and their subconscious content are generated spontaneously in the course of execution and frequently suggest titles to her. Of this work she has said: "The picture developed (bit by bit while I was working on it) into shapes symbolic of an exuberant figure and ladder, therefore *Jacob's Ladder*. (A favorite picture of mine in the Prado is Ribera's *Dream of Jacob*.)"

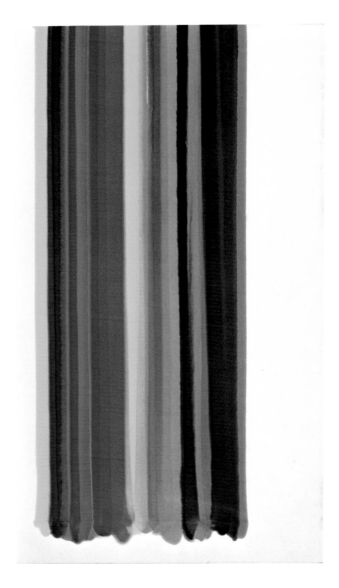

MORRIS LOUIS. American, 1912–1962. *Third Element.*
1962. Synthetic polymer paint on canvas, 7 feet 1¾
inches x 51 inches. Blanchette Rockefeller Fund. [200.63]

Morris Louis and his friend Kenneth Noland (page 37)
began to experiment with soak-staining unprimed canvas
after they had seen works by Helen Frankenthaler while
on a visit to New York in 1953. The technique and the
possibilities it opened up led Louis to abandon his previous Cubist-derived style and develop in a wholly independent way his exceptional gifts as a colorist. Instead of
creating cursive, expressionist shapes, such as those in
Frankenthaler's *Jacob's Ladder,* which bear the traces of
the artist's gesture and evoke associations with objects in
the real world, Louis evolved a type of configuration that
bespeaks nothing but the supremacy of color itself as an
optical reality.

In his "veil" paintings of the 'fifties, Louis allowed
successive waves of pigment to flow into and over one
another in loosely defined, fluctuating shapes. He chose
a type of synthetic paint that could be diluted almost to
the consistency of watercolor and still retain its transparency, even when several layers were superimposed.
The *Third Element,* however, is one of a number of
"stripe" paintings that preoccupied him just before his
death. Straight, vertical bands of varying thicknesses,
ranging from bright yellow to black, are grouped together and placed asymmetrically. Against the areas of

raw canvas left bare at the sides and below, the colors
seem disembodied, as though a curtain of tinted light
were suspended from the top of the picture, to fall to an
undulating edge a few inches above the bottom.

The critic Clement Greenberg has written of such
paintings: "The configurations . . . are not meant as images and do not act as images; they are far too abstract.
They are there to organize the picture field into elo-
quence. . . . Louis is not interested in veils or stripes as
such, but in verticality and color. . . . And yet the color,
the verticality . . . are not there for their own sakes. They
are there, first and foremost, for the sake of feeling, and
as vehicles of feeling. And if these paintings fail as
vehicles and expressions of feeling, they fail entirely."

141

ROBERT MOTHERWELL. American, born 1915. *Elegy to the Spanish Republic, 108*. 1965-1967. Oil on canvas, 6 feet 10 inches x 11 feet 6¼ inches. Purchase. [155.70]

Motherwell began painting his Spanish Elegies in 1949 and has since developed the theme in more than a hundred pictures, of which the *Elegy to the Spanish Republic, 108* is among the largest and most recent. For young intellectuals of his generation, the Spanish Civil War precipitated a moral crisis in the late 'thirties somewhat like that induced by the Vietnam War in the 'sixties and 'seventies. Motherwell declares, however, that his series of Elegies is not narrowly topical but is meant to have a wider significance: "I take an elegy to be a lamentation or funeral song for something one cared about. The 'Spanish Elegies' are not 'political' but my private insistence that a terrible death had happened that should not be forgot. They are as eloquent as I could make them. But the pictures are also general metaphors of the contrast between life and death, and their interrelation."

Early in his career, Motherwell was in close contact with artists in exile in the United States during the Second World War, including a number of Surrealists. Their emphasis upon automatism encouraged Motherwell to base his imagery upon free association. This applied not only to shapes but also to color—ocher, for example, symbolizing earth, and green, grass. The principal agents in the Spanish Elegies are black and white, representing the opposition and interrelation between death and anxiety, life and radiance.

In formal terms, the paintings of this series have in common their structural arrangement of irregularly ovoid shapes abutting vertical bars or rectangles of various widths. At the most elementary level, they may be read simply as composed of contrasting, basically geometrical forms. The shapes nevertheless evoke associations of male and female genitalia; it has also been suggested that they may refer indirectly to the phallus and testicles of the sacrificial bull hung up on the wall of the ring after a *corrida*.

Though Motherwell, like other Abstract Expressionists, sometimes makes use of accidental effects, in general his compositions are strictly controlled, depending on the precise relationships between the forms and their arrangement on the flat surface of the canvas, the rhythms established by the spatial intervals, and the interaction of the colors—especially their power to give off light (or, in the case of black, absorb and negate it). The mat surfaces of the Elegies add to the sense of austerity conveyed by their somber color and simple, rugged shapes.

ADOLPH GOTTLIEB. American, 1903–1974. *Blast, I.* 1957. Oil on canvas, 7 feet 6 inches x 45⅛ inches. Philip Johnson Fund. [6.58]

The *Blast, I,* like Motherwell's *Elegy to the Spanish Republic, 108,* belongs to a series in which the artist, by utilizing a few basic elements that are repeated with variations from one painting to another, explores the possibilities inherent within self-imposed limits. This is one of the earliest of Gottlieb's Burst paintings, which are composed of two contrasting forms placed one above the other—a dark, jagged shape below and a bright disk above. Unlike the forms in Motherwell's Elegies, these shapes, arranged on the vertical rather than the horizontal axis, are not tangent to each other or to the edge of the picture. Instead of appearing to be locked into position, they seem to float on the surface of the canvas, imparting to it a sense of energy and flux.

Whereas color, other than black and white, is secondary for Motherwell and chosen for its symbolism, Gottlieb used it for its emotional quality, as a primary vehicle of feeling: "I want to express the utmost intensity of color, bring out the quality, make it expressive. At the same time, I would like to bring out a certain immateriality that it can have, so that it exists as sensation." In *Blast, I,* this immateriality is especially evident in the treatment of the red disk, which is surrounded by a semitransparent halo that suggests rays emanating from a source of light.

Gottlieb always denied that the two abstract signs in his Burst paintings had any specific symbolism, but he took no doctrinaire position against the spectator's investing them with whatever meaning they may convey to him. "Paint quality is meaningless if it does not express quality of feeling," he declared. "Subjective images do not have to have rational association, but the act of painting must be rational, objective, and consciously disciplined." He applied the word "polarities" to his concept of the opposing shapes in the Burst pictures. Thus, one may see in them the dichotomies of light and dark (which, as in Motherwell's Elegies, may connote life and death), round and jagged, concentric and centrifugal, contraction and expansion, color and non-color.

143

BARNETT NEWMAN. American, 1905–1970. *Vir Heroicus Sublimis.* 1950–1951. Oil on canvas, 7 feet 11⅜ inches x 17 feet 9¼ inches. Gift of Mr. and Mrs. Ben Heller. [240.69]

The chief impression one has on first encountering this painting is probably that of its sheer size. Like Pollock's *One* (page 139), it functions like a mural, yet without reference to any architectural setting; there are no recognizable images or incidents to differentiate the parts of the painting, no frame to mark its borders. Its vast expanse becomes the viewer's environment and thus engages him in direct, intimate contact.

The huge canvas serves as vehicle for the red with which it is evenly covered from edge to edge. All that "happens" is the division of the area by five vertical stripes of different colors and widths, extending from top to bottom. Newman called these vertical stripes "zips"; like Mondrian (page 39), he established their positions by affixing tapes to his canvas. In the *Vir Heroicus Sublimis,* the exact center of the painting is occupied by an eight-foot square, while the remainder of the surface to left and right is asymmetrically divided.

In spite of the rigid discipline with which the elements of the composition are ordered, Newman vehemently espoused the idea that art must free itself from what he called "this death image, the grip of geometry.... Painting, like passion, is a living voice, which, when I hear it, I must speak, unfettered." A key to his intentions as an artist may be found in an essay he wrote several years before he painted the *Vir Heroicus Sublimis,* the first of his very large works: "The subject matter of creation is chaos.... The present painter can be said to work with chaos not only in the sense that he is handling the chaos of the blank picture plane but also in that he is handling the chaos of form. In trying to go beyond the visible and known world he is ... engaged in a true act of discovery in the creation of new forms and symbols that will have the living quality of creation.... In his will to set down the ordered truth, that is the expression of his attitude toward the mystery of life and death, it can be said that the artist like a true creator is delving in chaos. It is precisely this that makes him an artist for the Creator in creating the world began with the same material, for the artist tries to wrest truth from the void." (Compare Klee: "Art is a parable of Creation," page 98.)

The title of this painting, with its reference to man's sublime and heroic nature, is in itself an affirmation of Newman's somewhat mystical sense of the human condition with all its tragedy and dignity.

144

FRANK STELLA. American, born 1936. *Tuftonboro, IV.* 1966. Fluorescent alkyd and epoxy paint on canvas, 8 feet 4⅛ inches x 9 feet ¾ inch. Gift of David Whitney. [577.70]

Tuftonboro, IV is one of Stella's Irregular Polygons, a series that he began painting in 1965 on the basis of sketches going back to 1962. The works in this series have a common structure, built on three kinds of contrast: between two interpenetrating geometrical shapes; between the colors used in the reinforcing bands; and between mat and glossy pigment. Each of the eleven forms of Irregular Polygons has four versions that repeat the same pattern in different colors. In the Tuftonboro group, a triangle intersects a rectangle, truncated at the upper right.

Instead of making his bands of color contiguous, Stella created "breathing spaces" by separating them with narrow strips of tape; before removing the tape, he allowed the thinners in his paint to eat into it and create slightly irregular edges. He did this to avoid the hard, brittle, mechanical quality of conventional geometrical or hardedge painting and cites what may seem a surprising precedent: "I think what I had in mind in connection with these spaces was the example of Matisse—in something

like *The Red Studio* [page 74]. . . . The necessity of separating the colors, that breathing, that soft ground, and that identification of color with ground seemed very important to me."

Though other modern artists had departed from the traditional rectangular or circular support for their paintings, Stella was the first to make the irregular shape of his support coincide with the pattern painted upon it. Since he initiated this device in about 1960, many other artists have followed his lead and created "shaped canvases." Their palpable reality emphasizes their existence as tangible objects, not depictions of other objects.

The youngest of the artists represented in this book, Stella typifies the detached, "cool" generation of the 'sixties, in reaction against the "romanticism" of the Abstract Expressionists. He approaches painting in terms of problem-solving: "All I want anyone to get out of my paintings . . . is the fact that you can see the whole idea without any confusion. . . . What you see is what you see." To exclude "interpretation" is nevertheless not to deny sensuous pleasure: "But the worthwhile qualities of painting are always going to be both visual and emotional, and it's got to be a convincing emotional experience. Otherwise, it will not be a good—not to say, great—painting."

145

MARCEL DUCHAMP. American, born France, 1887–1968. Active in New York 1915–1918, 1920–1923, 1942–1968. *To Be Looked At* (*From the Other Side of the Glass*), *with One Eye, Close To, for Almost an Hour.* 1918. Oil paint, silver leaf, lead wire, lens on glass (cracked), between two panes of glass framed in metal, $20\frac{1}{8}$ x $16\frac{1}{4}$ inches. Katherine S. Dreier Bequest. [150.53]

In direct contrast to the approach of Stella (page 145), as epitomized in his flat statement, "My painting is based on the fact that only what can be seen there *is* there," is the position of Duchamp, who while still in his twenties determined to get away from the physicality of painting and create works that would appeal to the intellect rather than to the retina.

The *To Be Looked At* is a study for the upper right-hand section in the lower half of Duchamp's "Large Glass," *The Bride Stripped Bare by Her Bachelors, Even*—the culminating work in his preoccupation with the theme dealt with in *The Passage from Virgin to Bride* (page 56). While the *To Be Looked At* thus goes back to ideas with which he had been concerned since 1912, it also marks the beginning of his growing interest in the study of optics, which he was to pursue in the 'twenties. (If such an interest seems to run counter to his scorn for the "retinal," this is only one among the innumerable paradoxes that abound in Duchamp's activities.)

The portion of the Large Glass for which this is a study is devoted to the "oculist witnesses" of the Bride's disrobing. Typical of Duchamp's fondness for puns is the fact that *témoins oculistes* is also the French term for "eye charts." Besides being an instruction to the voyeurs of the anticipated titillating event, the full title *To Be Looked At* (*From the Other Side of the Glass*), *with One Eye, Close To, for Almost an Hour,* which is written on the diagonal bar, was also meant to sound like an oculist's prescription. Compliance with this direction by gazing fixedly through the magnifying lens attached to the glass would produce hallucinatory experiences like those provoked by Duchamp's optical machines—one of which, *Rotary Demisphere* (*Precision Optics*) of 1925, is owned by The Museum of Modern Art.

Another kind of optical effect in the *To Be Looked At* is created by the overlapping of the parallel red, yellow, blue, and green lines in the pyramid. Instead of appearing continuous, they seem to break at the angles of intersection. Duchamp created still a further illusion, that of three-dimensional depth, by using scientifically studied perspective to render the pyramid, the obelisk shape below the lens, and the rays that fan out around its base. He said, however, that he actually wished the Large Glass to be a kind of projection of the fourth dimension, which is invisible because the eye cannot perceive it.

The most novel feature of the *To Be Looked At,* of course, is that like *The Bride Stripped Bare by Her Bachelors, Even,* it is painted on glass. With this innovation, Duchamp not only did away with the conventional background for a painting but also provided one that changes according to what is seen through and beyond it. The work of art, therefore, does not create an environment for the spectator, as do Monet's *Water Lilies* (pages 24–25) and more recent wall-size paintings such as Newman's *Vir Heroicus Sublimis* (page 144). Instead, the environment itself is absorbed by, and becomes part of, the work of art, whose transparency makes it subject to constant change and the laws of chance. The breaking of this glass, and of *The Bride Stripped Bare,* were accidents that Duchamp had not foreseen; nevertheless, in the case of the latter happening, at least, he expressed delight both at the aesthetic effect produced by the silvery cracks and at the intervention of chance in his work.

The cultivation of chance and accident in art is only one of the ideas from Duchamp's inexhaustible store that has continued to stimulate artists to this day. Among many others, we may mention his efforts to construct metaphors for abstract ideas and for processes that take place in time, and his elevation to the status of art of "found" objects, which he called "Ready-mades." (The environments of his paintings on glass are in themselves a kind of Ready-made.) But undoubtedly Duchamp's most important contribution is his incessant challenging of all the usual assumptions about life and art, which forces artists and the public alike to a continual reappraisal of accepted values.

SELECTED BIBLIOGRAPHY

THIS BIBLIOGRAPHY includes books and catalogues issued by The Museum of Modern Art that relate to artists or tendencies represented in *An Invitation To See*. All publications listed are currently in print or are available in reprint editions. Dates are given for the original publications, which may be found in many libraries, including that of The Museum of Modern Art; many of them contain color plates, most of which appear only as black-and-white reproductions in the reprints.

In addition, special mention should be made of *Masters of Modern Art*, edited by Alfred H. Barr, Jr. and published on the occasion of the Museum's Twenty-fifth Anniversary in 1954. Though long out of print, it is readily available in libraries and is especially recommended for its valuable information on the Museum's collections and its many illustrations, including large color plates. Currently in print are a new and completely revised edition of *Painting and Sculpture in The Museum of Modern Art*, edited by Alfred H. Barr, Jr., which catalogues the 2,622 works acquired from 1929 to 1967 and contains 1,693 illustrations, and a paperbound checklist of the Painting and Sculpture Collection as of January 1, 1977, edited by Alicia Legg and incorporating 550 acquisitions of the intervening decade.

AMERICANS 1942-1963: *Six Group Exhibitions*, edited by Dorothy C. Miller, with statements by the artists and others. Arno Press reprint includes *Americans 1942; Fourteen Americans,* 1946; *15 Americans,* 1952; *12 Americans,* 1956; *Sixteen Americans,* 1959; and *Americans 1963.* 560 pages; 547 illustrations.

ART IN PROGRESS: *A Survey Prepared for the Fifteenth Anniversary of The Museum of Modern Art.* 1944. Arno Press reprint: 256 pages; 133 illustrations of paintings.

ART NOUVEAU: *Art and Design at the Turn of the Century,* edited by Peter Selz and Mildred Constantine, with articles by Greta Daniel, Alan M. Fern, Henry-Russell Hitchcock, and Peter Selz. 1959. Revised edition, 1975: 200 pages, 195 illustrations (8 in color).

ART OF THE TWENTIES, by William S. Lieberman. 1979. 144 pages; 250 illustrations.

BAUHAUS: 1919-1928, edited by Herbert Bayer, Walter Gropius, and Ise Gropius. 1938. Paperbound reprint, 1975: 224 pages, 550 illustrations.

CONTEMPORARY PAINTERS, by James Thrall Soby. 1948. Arno Press reprint: 152 pages, 65 illustrations.

CUBISM AND ABSTRACT ART, by Alfred H. Barr, Jr. 1936. Paperbound edition, 1974: 248 pages, 223 illustrations.

DADA, SURREALISM, AND THEIR HERITAGE, by William Rubin. 1968. Paperbound edition: 252 pages, 300 illustrations.

EUROPEAN MASTER PAINTINGS FROM SWISS COLLECTIONS: *Post-Impressionism to World War II,* by John Elderfield. 1976. 172 pages; 72 illustrations (24 in color).

FANTASTIC ART, DADA, SURREALISM, edited by Alfred H. Barr, Jr., with essays by Georges Hugnet. 1936. Arno Press reprint of 3rd edition, revised, 1947: 284 pages; 222 illustrations.

GERMAN ART OF THE TWENTIETH CENTURY, by Werner Haftmann, Alfred Hentzen, and William S. Lieberman; edited by Andrew Carnduff Ritchie. 1957. Arno Press reprint: 240 pages; 185 illustrations.

THE HISTORY OF IMPRESSIONISM, by John Rewald. 1946. Revised and enlarged edition, 1973: 672 pages; 623 illustrations (82 in color).

THE MEANINGS OF MODERN ART, by John Russell. 1974-1975. 12 volumes, each 48 pages, 62 illustrations (12 in color). Issued in association with the Book-of-the-Month Club.

MODERN GERMAN PAINTING AND SCULPTURE, with introduction and notes by Alfred H. Barr, Jr. 1931. Arno Press reprint: 94 pages; 50 illustrations.

MODERN MASTERS: *Manet to Matisse,* edited by William S. Lieberman. 1975. 272 pages; 129 illustrations (16 in color).

THE NEW AMERICAN PAINTING as Shown in Eight European Countries, 1958-1959, with introduction by Alfred H. Barr, Jr. 1959. Arno Press reprint: 96 pages; 86 illustrations.

POST-IMPRESSIONISM: *From van Gogh to Gauguin,* by John Rewald. 3rd, revised edition, 1978: 592 pages; 534 illustrations (50 in color).

THE SCHOOL OF PARIS: *Paintings from the Florene May Schoenborn and Samuel A. Marx Collection.* Preface by Alfred H. Barr, Jr., introduction by James Thrall Soby, notes by Lucy Lippard. 1965. Paperbound reprint, 1979: 56 pages, 46 illustrations (16 in color).

THREE GENERATIONS OF TWENTIETH-CENTURY ART: *The Sidney and Harriet Janis Collection of The Museum of Modern Art,* with foreword by Alfred H. Barr, Jr. and introduction by William Rubin. 1972. 252 pages; 157 illustrations (17 in color).

TWENTIETH-CENTURY ITALIAN ART, by James Thrall Soby and Alfred H. Barr, Jr. 1949. Arno Press reprint: 144 pages; 143 illustrations.

WHAT IS MODERN PAINTING?, by Alfred H. Barr, Jr. Reprint, 1975, of 9th edition, revised, 1966: 48 pages; 64 illustrations (2 in color).

THE "WILD BEASTS": *Fauvism and Its Affinities,* by John Elderfield. 1976. 168 pages; 206 illustrations (24 in color).

INDIVIDUAL ARTISTS

ARP, edited by James Thrall Soby, with essays by Jean Hans Arp and Richard Huelsenbeck. 1956. Arno Press reprint: 128 pages, 114 illustrations.

MAX BECKMANN, by Peter Selz, with contributions by Perry T. Rathbone and Harold Joachim. 1964. Arno Press reprint: 160 pages; 113 illustrations.

CÉZANNE: *The Late Work,* edited by William Rubin, with essays by Theodore Reff, Lawrence Gowing, Liliane Brion-Guerry, John Rewald, F. Novotny, Geneviève Monnier, Douglas Druick, George Heard Hamilton, and William Rubin; catalogue by John Rewald. 1977. 416 pages, 427 illustrations (50 in color).

CÉZANNE, GAUGUIN, SEURAT, VAN GOGH: *First Loan Exhibition,* by Alfred H. Barr, Jr. 1929. Arno Press reprint: 150 pages; 97 illustrations.

MARC CHAGALL, by James Johnson Sweeney. 1946. Arno Press reprint: 102 pages; 81 illustrations.

GIORGIO DE CHIRICO, by James Thrall Soby. 1955. Arno Press reprint: 268 pages; 194 illustrations.

SALVADOR DALI, *Paintings, Drawings, Prints,* by James Thrall Soby. 1941. Arno Press reprint of 2nd revised edition, 1946: 112 pages; 80 illustrations.

STUART DAVIS, by James Johnson Sweeney. 1945. Arno Press reprint (included in *Three American Modernist Painters*): 40 pages; 31 illustrations.

CHARLES DEMUTH, by Andrew Carnduff Ritchie. 1950. Arno Press reprint: 96 pages, 70 illustrations.

THE WORK OF JEAN DUBUFFET, by Peter Selz, with texts by the artist. 1962. Arno Press reprint: 188 pages, 125 illustrations.

MARCEL DUCHAMP, edited by Anne d'Harnoncourt and Kynaston McShine. 1973. 360 pages; 429 illustrations (12 in color).

JAMES ENSOR, by Libby Tannenbaum. 1951. Arno Press reprint: 128 pages; 110 illustrations.

MAX ERNST, edited by William S. Lieberman, including "An Informal Life of M.E. (as told by himself to a young friend)." 1961. Arno Press reprint: 66 pages; 85 illustrations.

LYONEL FEININGER, with essays by Alois J. Schardt, Alfred H. Barr, Jr.; edited by Dorothy C. Miller. 1944. Arno Press reprint (included in *Feininger-Hartley*): 52 pages; 49 illustrations.

GAUGUIN, *see* CÉZANNE, GAUGUIN, SEURAT, VAN GOGH

VINCENT VAN GOGH, with an introduction and notes selected from the letters of the artist, edited by Alfred H. Barr, Jr. 1935. Arno Press reprint of 3rd edition, 1936, emended: 194 pages; 88 illustrations.

VAN GOGH, *see also* CÉZANNE, GAUGUIN, SEURAT, VAN GOGH

ARSHILE GORKY, *Paintings, Drawings, Studies,* by William C. Seitz; foreword by Julien Levy. 1962. Arno Press reprint: 56 pages; 85 illustrations.

JUAN GRIS, by James Thrall Soby. 1958. Arno Press reprint: 128 pages, 126 illustrations.

HANS HOFMANN, by William C. Seitz. 1963. Arno Press reprint: 64 pages; 47 illustrations.

EDWARD HOPPER, with texts by Alfred H. Barr, Jr. and Charles Burchfield. 1933. Arno Press reprint (included in *Three Painters of America*): 84 pages, 49 illustrations.

PAUL KLEE: *Three Exhibitions, 1930, 1941, 1949.* Arno Press reprint includes *Paul Klee,* with introduction by Alfred H. Barr, Jr., 1930; *Paul Klee,* with statements by the artist and articles by Alfred H. Barr, Jr., Julia and Lyonel Feininger, and James Johnson Sweeney, 2nd edition, revised, 1945; *Paintings, Drawings, and Prints by Paul Klee from the Klee Foundation, Berne, Switzerland, with additions from American Collections,* with introduction by James Thrall Soby, 1949. 160 pages, 109 illustrations.

LAUTREC-REDON: *Tenth Loan Exhibition,* by Jere Abbott. 1931. Arno Press reprint: 72 pages; 39 illustrations.

JOHN MARIN, with essays by Henry McBride, Marsden Hartley, and E. M. Benson. 1936. Arno Press reprint: 104 pages; 49 illustrations.

MATISSE: *His Art and His Public,* by Alfred H. Barr, Jr. 1951. Paperbound reprint, 1974: 610 pages, 508 illustrations (8 in color).

Matisse in the Collection of The Museum of Modern Art, by John Elderfield, with additional commentaries by William S. Lieberman and Riva Castleman. 1978. 232 pages, 274 illustrations (34 in color).

Joan Miró, by James Thrall Soby. 1959. Arno Press reprint: 164 pages, 148 illustrations.

Joan Miró, by James Johnson Sweeney. 1941. Arno Press reprint: 88 pages, 71 illustrations.

Miró in the Collection of The Museum of Modern Art, by William Rubin 1973. 140 pages; 157 illustrations (22 in color).

Modigliani: *Paintings, Drawings, Sculpture,* introduction by James Thrall Soby. 1951. Arno Press reprint: 56 pages; 42 illustrations.

Claude Monet: *Seasons and Moments,* by William C. Seitz. 1960. Arno Press reprint: 64 pages, 44 illustrations.

Emil Nolde, by Peter Selz. 1963. Arno Press reprint: 88 pages, 67 illustrations.

Picasso: *Fifty Years of His Art,* by Alfred H. Barr, Jr. 1946. Paperbound reprint, 1974: 316 pages, 338 illustrations (8 in color).

Picasso in the Collection of The Museum of Modern Art, by William Rubin, with additional texts by Elaine L. Johnson and Riva Castleman. 1972. 248 pages; 307 illustrations (49 in color).

Redon, *see* Lautrec-Redon.

Diego Rivera, with introduction by Frances Flynn Paine, notes by Jere Abbott. 1931. Arno Press reprint: 128 pages; 75 illustrations.

Mark Rothko, by Peter Selz. 1961. Arno Press reprint: 44 pages; 29 illustrations.

Georges Rouault: *Paintings and Prints,* by James Thrall Soby. 1945. Arno Press reprint of 3rd edition. 1947: 142 pages; 131 illustrations.

Henri Rousseau, by Daniel Catton Rich. 1942. Arno Press reprint of 2nd edition, revised, 1946: 80 pages; 53 illustrations.

Seurat, *see* Cézanne, Gauguin, Seurat, van Gogh

Charles Sheeler: *Paintings, Drawings, Photographs,* with introduction by William Carlos Williams. 1939. Arno Press reprint (in *Three Painters of America*): 54 pages, 31 illustrations.

Soutine, by Monroe Wheeler. 1950. Arno Press reprint: 116 pages; 78 illustrations.

Yves Tanguy, by James Thrall Soby. 1955. Arno Press reprint: 72 pages; 59 illustrations.

Tchelitchew: *Paintings, Drawings,* by James Thrall Soby. 1942. Arno Press reprint: 100 pages; 80 illustrations.

Mark Tobey, by William C. Seitz. 1962. Arno Press reprint: 112 pages, 86 illustrations.

Édouard Vuillard, by Andrew Carnduff Ritchie. 1954. Arno Press reprint: 104 pages; 91 illustrations.

ACKNOWLEDGMENTS AND SOURCES

MY FIRST THANKS go to the staff of the Museum's information desk and bookstores, whose unremitting reports over many years of the public's demand for material on the collections were a special incentive for writing this book. I am grateful to Richard E. Oldenburg, Director of the Museum, for entrusting me with the task, and to Carl Morse, Editor-in-Chief, for providing constant encouragement and valuable editorial advice. The selection of paintings for inclusion was made in consultation with William Rubin, Chief Curator of the Painting and Sculpture Collection, and William S. Lieberman, Chief Curator of Drawings; Mr. Rubin also graciously made available the typescript of a monograph on Abstract Expressionism that he has in preparation. Betsy Jones, Curator of Painting and Sculpture, kindly read the entire manuscript; her unparalleled knowledge of the collection and scrupulous accuracy eliminated a number of factual errors. Jillian Slonim, while an intern in the Department of Publications, did preliminary research on some of the sources quoted; Frances Keech, Permissions Editor, assembled the data for the bibliography. Carl Laanes brought enthusiasm as well as skill to solving the problems of design. With his customary good humor and efficiency, Jack Doenias, aided by his assistants Karen Chervin and Francesca Cinelli, supervised all details of production and saw the book through the press.

—H.M.F.

GRATEFUL ACKNOWLEDGMENT is made to the sources listed below for the use of quotations on the pages indicated:

p. 8. Christian Zervos, "Conversation avec Picasso," *Cahiers d'Art* (Paris), vol. 10, 1935, pp. 173–78, quoted in English translation in Alfred H. Barr, Jr., *Picasso: Fifty Years of His Art,* New York, The Museum of Modern Art, 1946, p. 274.

p. 10. Letter of van Gogh to his brother Theo, found on his person July 29, 1890, published in English translation in *Further Letters of Vincent van Gogh to His Brother,* London, Constable & Co., Boston & New York, Houghton Mifflin, 1929, p. 488.—Henri Matisse, "Notes of a Painter" (1908), published in English translation in Alfred H. Barr, Jr., *Matisse: His Art and His Public,* New York, The Museum of Modern Art, 1951, p. 122.—Marcel Duchamp, "The Creative Act," speech delivered at convention of the American Federation of Arts, Houston, published in *Art News* (New York), vol. 56, Summer 1957, pp. 28–29.—Leo Steinberg, "Contemporary Art and the Plight of Its Public," based on a lecture given at The Museum of Modern Art, New York, Spring 1960, first published in *Harper's Magazine* (New York), March

1962, reprinted in Leo Steinberg, *Other Criteria: Confrontations with Twentieth-Century Art,* New York, Oxford University Press, 1972, pp. 10, 15–16.—Marianne Moore, "When I Buy Pictures," reprinted with permission of Macmillan Publishing Co., Inc., from *Collected Poems of Marianne Moore,* copyright 1935 by Marianne Moore, renewed 1963 by Marianne Moore and T. S. Eliot.

p. 13. Letter of Henri Rousseau to the Mayor of Laval, published in *Le Petit Journal* (Paris), Jan. 7, 1935, quoted in English translation by Daniel Catton Rich, *Henri Rousseau,* 2nd edition, New York, The Museum of Modern Art, 1946, p. 31.—Jean Cocteau, catalogue of sale of the John Quinn Collection, Hôtel Drouot, Paris, Oct. 28, 1925, quoted in English translation in *Masters of Modern Art,* edited by Alfred H. Barr, Jr., New York, The Museum of Modern Art, 1954, p. 13.

p. 15. Barr, *Masters of Modern Art,* p. 30.

p. 19. Marius-Ary Leblond, catalogue of the exhibition "van Dongen," Paris, Bernheim-Jeune, 1908.

p. 20. James Ensor, speech at exhibition of his works, Jeu de Paume, Paris, June 1932, published in English translation in Paul Haesaerts, *James Ensor,* New York, Harry N. Abrams, 1959, p. 357.

p. 21. *Klee (1879–1940),* with an introduction and notes by Andrew Forge, London, Faber and Faber, 1954, vol. 2, p. 12.

p. 25. Alfred H. Barr, Jr., exhibition gallery label, The Museum of Modern Art, 1959.

p. 26. Edmond Duranty, "La Nouvelle peinture" (1876), quoted in English translation in John Russell, catalogue of the exhibition "Édouard Vuillard," Art Gallery of Toronto, Sept. 11–Oct. 24, 1971, p. 18.

p. 32. František Kupka, quoted in article by W. Warshawky, "Orpheism (*sic*), Latest of Painting Cults," *New York Times,* Oct. 19, 1913.

p. 33. From Delaunay's notebooks, 1939–1940, quoted in Robert Delaunay, *Du Cubisme à l'art abstrait,* edited by Pierre Francastel, Paris, S.E.V.P.E.N., 1957, p. 81.

p. 34. Josef Albers, quoted by Kynaston L. McShine in catalogue of the exhibition "Josef Albers: Homage to the Square," organized by The International Council of The Museum of Modern Art, 1964.—Reply to a questionnaire in the Collection files of The Museum of Modern Art.

p. 35. Mark Rothko, lecture given at Pratt Institute, Brooklyn, 1958, edited by Dore Ashton, *Cimaise* (Paris), Dec. 1958, p. 39, quoted in catalogue of the exhibition "New York School: The First Generation," Los Angeles

County Museum of Art, July 16–Aug. 1, 1965, p. 30.

p. 36. Kasimir Malevich, "From Cubism and Futurism to Suprematism: The New Realism in Painting," *Essays on Art 1915–1928,* translated by Xenia Glowacki-Prus and Arnold McMillin, edited by Troels Andersen, Copenhagen, Borgen, 1968, p. 38, p. 24.

p. 38. Piet Mondrian, "The New Plastic as 'Abstract-Real Painting': The Plastic Means and Composition," *De Stijl,* vol. 1, no. 3, 1917, quoted in Hans L. C. Jaffé, *De Stijl,* New York, Harry N. Abrams, 1970, p. 54.

p. 39. Quoted by James Johnson Sweeney, "Eleven Europeans in America," *Museum of Modern Art Bulletin,* vol. 13, 1946, p. 36.

p. 40. Wassily Kandinsky, *Rückblicken,* Berlin, Herwarth Walden, 1913, quoted in English translation in *Modern Artists on Art,* edited by Robert L. Herbert, Englewood Cliffs, N.J., Prentice-Hall, 1964, p. 32.

p. 42. Letter of Serge I. Shchukin to Henri Matisse, March 31, 1909, quoted in English translation in Barr, *Matisse: His Art and His Public,* p. 133.

p. 44. Picabia as paraphrased in an interview by Hutchins Hapgood, "A Paris Painter," *The Globe and Commercial Adviser* (New York), Feb. 20, 1913, p. 8, reprinted in *Camera Work* (New York), nos. 42–43, April–July 1913, pp. 50, 51.

p. 45. Information from reply to a questionnaire in the Collection file of The Museum of Modern Art.

pp. 46–47. Leo Steinberg, "The Philosophical Brothel," Part II, *Art News* (New York), vol. 71, Oct. 1972, pp. 39, 43, 45, 46.—Barr, *Picasso: Fifty Years of His Art,* p. 56.

p. 53. Robert Rosenblum, *Cubism and Twentieth-Century Art,* New York, Harry N. Abrams, 1961, p. 241.

p. 54. Marianne W. Martin, *Futurist Art and Theory, 1909–1915,* Oxford, Clarendon Press, 1968, p. 158.—Futurist Painting: Technical Manifesto, quoted in English translation in Joshua C. Taylor, *Futurism,* New York, The Museum of Modern Art, 1961, pp. 125–126.—"The Exhibitors to the Public," on the occasion of the Futurist exhibition at Bernheim-Jeune, Paris, Feb. 5–12, 1912, quoted in English translation in Taylor, *ibid.,* p. 128.

p. 56. Quoted by James Johnson Sweeney, "Eleven Europeans in America," p. 20.—Letter from Marcel Duchamp to Alfred H. Barr, Jr., Feb. 21, 1963, in Collection files of The Museum of Modern Art.

p. 58. "Kurt Schwitters Katalog," *Merz 20* (Hanover), March 1927, quoted in English translation in William S. Rubin, *Dada, Surrealism, and Their Heritage,* New York, The Museum of Modern Art, 1968, p. 54.—Kurt Schwitters, "Merz" (1920), reprinted in English translation in *The Dada Painters and Poets,* edited by Robert Motherwell, New York, Wittenborn, Schultz, 1951, p. 57.

p. 59. Alfred H. Barr, Jr., *What Is Modern Painting?,* 6th edition, revised, New York, The Museum of Modern Art, 1966, p. 11.

p. 60. Reply to questionnaire in the Collection files of The Museum of Modern Art.

p. 62. Reply to questionnaire in the Collection files of The Museum of Modern Art.

p. 64. [Marie McSwigan] *Sky Hooks: The Autobiography of John Kane,* Philadelphia & New York, J. B. Lippincott, 1938, pp. 82, 101, 172.

p. 65. Quoted in English translation in Hugo Claus, *Karel Appel,* New York, Harry N. Abrams, 1962.

p. 68. Barr, *Matisse: His Art and His Public,* p. 174.

p. 71. Fernand Léger, letter to Alfred H. Barr, Jr., Nov. 20, 1943, in Collection files of The Museum of Modern Art.

p. 75. Harriet Janis, in Alfred H. Barr, Jr., *Cubism and Abstract Art,* New York, The Museum of Modern Art, 1936, opposite fig. 88.

p. 76. Marion Bernadik, cited in Alfred H. Barr, Jr., *Picasso: Fifty Years of His Art,* p. 176.

p. 77. Morris Hirshfield, "My Life Biography," in Sidney Janis, *They Taught Themselves: American Primitive Painters of the 20th Century,* New York, Dial Press, 1942, p. 18.

p. 78. James Thrall Soby, *Modigliani,* New York, The Museum of Modern Art, 1963, p. 11.

p. 80. Rousseau's poem translated by Bertha Ten Eyck James, in Daniel Catton Rich, *Henri Rousseau,* 2nd edition, New York, The Museum of Modern Art, p. 69.

p. 81. James Johnson Sweeney in catalogue of the exhibition "Wifredo Lam," University of Notre Dame Art Gallery, Notre Dame, Indiana, Jan. 8–29, 1961.

p. 82. Robert Goldwater, *Rufino Tamayo,* New York, Quadrangle Press, 1947, p. 7.

p. 83. Quoted by Sidney Janis in *Abstract & Surrealist Art in America,* New York, Reynal & Hitchcock, 1944, p. 112.

p. 84. Alfred H. Barr, Jr., exhibition gallery label, The Museum of Modern Art.—"Manuscript from Collection of the Late Paul Eluard," published in English translation as Appendix A in James Thrall Soby, *Giorgio de Chirico,* New York, The Museum of Modern Art, 1955, pp. 244, 247, 248, 245.—Soby, *ibid.,* pp. 51–52.

p. 86. Salvador Dali, *Conquest of the Irrational,* translated from the French by David Gascoyne, New York, Julien Levy, 1935, p. 12.

p. 87. "Some Data on the Youth of M.E. as Told by Himself," *View* (New York), ser. 2, no. 1, April 1942 (Max Ernst Number), p. 28.

p. 88. Jean (Hans) Arp, "Notes from a Diary," *Transition* (Paris), no. 21, 1932, p. 191.—Arp, "Looking," in *Arp,* edited by James Thrall Soby, New York, The Museum of Modern Art, 1958, p. 14.

p. 90. Quoted by James Thrall Soby in *Joan Miró,* New York, The Museum of Modern Art, 1959, p. 37.

p. 91. Reply to questionnaire in Collection files of The Museum of Modern Art.—William S. Rubin, *Dada and Surrealism,* New York, Harry N. Abrams, 1969, p. 348.

p. 92. James Thrall Soby, *Yves Tanguy,* New York, The Museum of Modern Art, 1955, p. 22.

p. 93. Information in a letter from Delvaux to Mrs. R. Hammacher, July 26, 1968 (copy in Collection files of The Museum of Modern Art).—Jules Verne, *A Journey to the Centre of the Earth,* New York, Dodd, Mead, 1959, pp. 1–3.

p. 94. Theodore Reff, "Redon's *Le Silence:* An Iconographic Interpretation," *Gazette des Beaux Arts* (Paris), ser. 6, vol. 70, Dec. 1967, pp. 359-68.

p. 96. John Szarkowski, *The Photographer's Eye,* New York, The Museum of Modern Art, 1966, pp. 8-9.—Letter from Giacomo Balla to Alfred H. Barr, Jr., April 24, 1954, in Collection files of The Museum of Modern Art.

p. 97. Lloyd Goodrich and Doris Bry, *Georgia O'Keeffe,* New York, Whitney Museum of American Art, 1970, p. 17.

p. 98. Paul Klee, *Schöpferische Konfession,* Berne, Klipstein & Kornfeld, 1956; English translation by Richard and Klara Winston, "Creative Confession," in Felix Klee, *Paul Klee: His Life and Works in Documents,* New York, George Braziller, 1962, pp. 154-55.

p. 100. Max Ernst, "An Informal Life of M.E. (as told by himself to a young friend)," in *Max Ernst,* edited by William S. Lieberman, New York, The Museum of Modern Art, 1961, p. 9.—Max Ernst, *Beyond Painting,* The Documents of Modern Art, New York, Wittenborn, Schultz, 1948, pp. 9, 11.—Ernst, "An Informal Life of M.E.," p. 10.

p. 101. Jasper Johns, quoted in *Time* magazine (New York), May 4, 1959, p. 58.—"Five Young Artists," *Charm* (New York), April 1959, p. 85, quoted in Leo Steinberg, *Jasper Johns,* New York, George Wittenborn, 1963, pp. 8, 10.

p. 102. Dorothy C. Miller, "Edwin Dickinson," in John I. H. Baur, ed., *New Art in America: Fifty Painters of the 20th Century,* Greenwich, Conn., New York Graphic Society, 1957, p. 216.

p. 103. Barr, *Masters of Modern Art,* p. 163.—Reply to questionnaire, and letter from Tchelitchew to a doctor in La Jolla, July 11, 1956, in Collection files of The Museum of Modern Art.

pp. 104-105. Max Beckmann, letter to Curt Valentin, February 11, 1938, published in English translation in Peter Selz, *Max Beckmann,* New York, The Museum of Modern Art, 1964, p. 61.—Quoted in *ibid.,* p. 58.

p. 106. James Thrall Soby, "Peter Blume's 'Eternal City,'" *Museum of Modern Art Bulletin,* vol. 10, Apr. 1943, pp. 3-6.

p. 108. Reply to questionnaire in Collection files of The Museum of Modern Art.

p. 109. Quoted by Frederick S. Wight, "A Jack Levine Profile," *Art Digest* (New York), Sept. 15, 1952, p. 10.

p. 112. Quoted by Van Deren Coke in catalogue of the exhibition "The Painter and the Photograph," The Art Gallery, University of New Mexico, Albuquerque, 1964, p. 32.

p. 113. Reply to questionnaire in Collection files of The Museum of Modern Art.—Quoted by Elizabeth McCausland, "Jacob Lawrence," *Magazine of Art* (Washington), vol. 38, Nov. 1945, p. 251.

p. 114. Marcel Nicolle in *Journal de Rouen,* 1905, quoted in English translation in Barr, *Matisse: His Art and His Public,* pp. 55.—Derain, letter to Vlaminck, quoted in English translation in Denys Sutton, *André Derain,* London, Phaidon, 1959, pp. 20, 19.

p. 115. Hans Hess, *Lyonel Feininger,* New York, Harry N. Abrams, 1961, p. 56.—*Ibid.,* p. 82.—Lyonel Feininger, letter to Alfred Kubin, Oct. 5, 1913, quoted in English translation in Hess, *ibid.,* p. 68.

p. 116. Barr, *Matisse: His Art and His Public,* p. 173.

p. 117. Henri Matisse, "Notes of a Painter" (1908), quoted in English translation in Barr, *Matisse: His Art and His Public,* pp. 119-21.—Clement Greenberg, *Arts Review* (London), vol. 14, Sept. 22-Oct. 6, 1962, p. 12.

p. 119. Charles Sheeler, quoted in Henry Geldzahler, *American Painting in the Twentieth Century,* New York, The Metropolitan Museum of Art, 1963, p. 139.

p. 120. Reply to questionnaire in Collection files of The Museum of Modern Art.

p. 121. Lloyd Goodrich, *Edward Hopper: Selections from the Hopper Bequest,* New York, Whitney Museum of American Art, 1971, pp. 9-10.

p. 122. Monroe Wheeler, *Soutine,* New York, The Museum of Modern Art, 1950, p. 50.—Jack Tworkov, "The Wandering Soutine," *Art News* (New York), vol. 49, Nov. 1950, pp. 32, 62.

p. 123. Barr, *Masters of Modern Art,* p. 114.—John Marin in catalogue of his one-man show at "291" Gallery, New York, 1913, reprinted in MacKinley Helm, *John Marin,* Boston, Pellegrini & Cudahy in association with Institute of Contemporary Art, 1948, pp. 28-29.

p. 124. Ludwig Kirchner, letter to Curt Valentin, 1937, quoted in Bernard Myers, *The German Expressionists,* New York, Frederick A. Praeger, 1957, p. 128.

p. 125. Jean Dubuffet, "Statement on Paintings of 1961," in Peter Selz, *The Work of Jean Dubuffet,* New York, The Museum of Modern Art, 1962, p. 165.—Letter from Dubuffet to H. Damisch, May 31, 1962, in *Catalogue des travaux de Jean Dubuffet,* edited by Max Loreau, fasc. 19. "Paris Circus," Paris, Jean-Jacques Pauvert, 1965, p. 57.

p. 126. Quoted by Katharine Kuh, *The Artist's Voice: Talks with Seventeen Artists,* New York and Evanston, Harper & Row, 1962, p. 52.—Information given by Stuart Davis in conversation with Alfred H. Barr, Jr., Nov. 3, 1952 (transcript in Collection files of The Museum of Modern Art).—Quoted by Kuh, *ibid.,* p. 56.

p. 127. Quoted by G. R. Swenson, "What Is Pop Art?," Part II, *Art News* (New York), vol. 62, Feb. 1964, p. 64.—Quoted in catalogue of the Wallraf-Richartz Museum exhibition "James Rosenquist," Kunsthalle, Cologne, Jan. 29-March 12, 1972, p. 38.

p. 128. John Coplans, "Roy Lichtenstein: An Interview," in catalogue of the exhibition "Roy Lichtenstein," Pasadena Art Museum, April 18-May 28, 1967, p. 16.— "Lichtenstein Interviewed by Diane Waldman," in Diane Waldman, *Roy Lichtenstein,* New York, Harry N. Abrams, 1971, p. 28.

p. 129. Quoted by James Johnson Sweeney, "Eleven Europeans in America," p. 15.

p. 130. Jean Dubuffet, "Landscaped Tables, Landscapes of the Mind, Stones of Philosophy," translated by the artist and Marcel Duchamp for catalogue of the exhibition of the same name, Pierre Matisse Gallery, New York, Feb. 12-March 1, 1952; reprinted in Selz, *Jean Dubuffet,* p. 64.

p. 131. Thomas B. Hess, "De Kooning Paints a Picture," *Art News* (New York), vol. 52, March 1953, p. 67.

p. 132. Quoted by Maria Luz, "Témoignages: Henri Matisse," *XXe Siècle* (Paris), no. 2, 1952; quoted in English translation by Monroe Wheeler, *The Last Works of Henri Matisse,* New York, The Museum of Modern Art, 1961, p. 10.

p. 133. Hans Hofmann, "Selected Writings on Art," unpublished typescript in the Library of The Museum of Modern Art, quoted by William C. Seitz, *Hans Hofmann,* New York, The Museum of Modern Art, 1963, p. 27.

p. 134. Benjamin Townsend, "An Interview with Clyfford Still," *Audit* (Buffalo), Winter/Spring 1961.

p. 135. Franz Kline, interview by David Sylvester, *Living Arts* (London), vol. I, Spring 1963, quoted by Maurice Tuchman in catalogue of the exhibition "New York School: The First Generation," Los Angeles County Museum of Art, July 16-Aug. 1, 1965, pp. 18-19.

p. 136. Quoted by Selden Rodman, *Conversations with Artists,* New York, Devin-Adair, 1957, p. 17.—Reply to questionnaire in Collection files of The Museum of Modern Art.

p. 138. Frank O'Hara, *Jackson Pollock,* New York, George Braziller, 1959, pp. 28-29.

p. 140. Reply to questionnaire in Collection files of The Museum of Modern Art.

p. 141. Clement Greenberg in catalogue of the exhibition "Three New American Painters, Louis, Noland, Olitski," Norman Mackenzie Art Gallery, Regina, Sask., Jan. 14-Feb. 15, 1963, reprinted in catalogue of the exhibition "Morris Louis 1912-1962," Museum of Fine Arts, Boston, 1965, p. 83.

p. 142. Robert Motherwell, "A Conversation at Lunch," in catalogue of the exhibition "Robert Motherwell," Smith College, Northampton, Mass., Jan. 1963.

p. 143. Adolph Gottlieb, taped interview by Martin Friedman, 1962, quoted by Robert Doty in catalogue of the exhibition "Adolph Gottlieb," Whitney Museum of American Art and Solomon R. Guggenheim Museum, New York, 1968, p. 21.—Statement in catalogue of the exhibition "The New Decade: 35 American Painters and Sculptors," Whitney Museum of American Art, May 11-Aug. 7, 1955, p. 36.

p. 144. Barnett Newman, statement (1958) in catalogue of the exhibition "The New American Painting as Seen in Eight European Countries," New York, The Museum of Modern Art, 1959, p. 36.—Barnett Newman, "The Plasmic Image, Part I, 1943-1945," in Thomas B. Hess, *Barnett Newman,* New York, The Museum of Modern Art, 1971, p. 38.

p. 145. Taped conversation with the artist, quoted by William S. Rubin, *Frank Stella,* New York, The Museum of Modern Art, 1970, p. 118.—Bruce Glaser, "Questions to Stella and Judd," edited by Lucy R. Lippard, *Art News* (New York), vol. 65, Sept. 1966, pp. 58-59.

PHOTOGRAPH CREDITS

INDEX